For more information, find CCM at:

http://copingmechanisms.net

THE

Poetics

SKY

of

ISN'T

Spaces

BLUE

.

JANICE

Essays

LEE

Earlier versions of select essays first appeared in *Entropy*.

for Sal,

Benny & Maggie,

and 엄마

In every manner of framing, there is a house.

There is a door one must enter through, a door one must shut behind herself in order to leave.

In every manner of space, there is an intimate and crucial rivalry between *open* and *close,* between *time* and *memory,* between *myself* and *yourself.* The further we walk together, the further we walk in parallel, that distance between us that wavers, minuscule on some days, and incredibly vast on others, but always and certainly *there,* that distance persists.

The entire sky *between* us.

The entire sky between *us.*

THE SALTON SEA

We all begin with the premise that the color of the sky is blue. But the sky knows how to not fall onto the ground below.

A restless perambulation on the threshold of being: this is the definition of a poem.

When we study a poem, we rewrite its intimacy with a space, the horizonless sky enclosed in language capsules.

Steeper.

Steeper, still.

Too, the murmur of a dead fish, the endless wonder locked in an image that is a thing in a place.

For me, there is something so significant and evident in the Salton Sea as a space.

Gaston Bachelard in *The Poetics of Space*: "The poet speaks on the threshold of being."

Then, quoting Pierre-Jean Jouve:

> Poetry, especially in its present endeavors, (can) only correspond to attentive thought that is enamored of something unknown, and essentially receptive to becoming.

The Salton Sea, as a place, becomes a strange sort of refuge, a sanctuary. The sublime experience of *being* in a place, the beckoning and conjuring, immutable and barely audible, acts of insinuation. For a non-religious person, this is the correspondence of a spiritual awakening, a poetic spirituality that can be found, *here*. Here: God, present, via the failure of language, the inarticulateable nature of the *being* in a place.

Morphability of voice.

The very trace in the air.

Increased breath.

Falling headlong into essence.

Extend your ear.

Again.

Again, that sense of endless wonder.

I have been going on these annual pilgrimages to the Salton
Sea. My first official pilgrimage was in 2012. It was 115 degrees
outside. A strange and nostalgic tune, Django Reinhardt, play-
ing out of the car's stereo. The thickness of the air. To step out of
the air-conditioned car, into the density of the heat, the burden
of silence, here, the retracing of a melancholic achievement, the
spectral acoustics of the sea, the localization of memories.

Arm outstretched.

House unfastened.

Dismay.

And hope.

Henri Bosco:
> There is nothing like silence to suggest a sense of unlimited
> space.

Gaston Bachelard:

> Memory—what a strange thing it is!—does not record
> concrete duration, in the Bergsonian sense of the word.
> We are unable to relieve duration that has been destroyed.
> We can only think of it, in the line of an abstract time that
> is deprived of all thickness. The finest specimens of fossil-
> ized duration concretized as a result of long sojourn, are
> to be found in and through space. The unconscious abides.
> Memories are motionless, and the more securely they are
> fixed in space, the sounder they are.

Here is a place that truly hovers between life and death. This
is living and dying. Home without a cellar. Heroism without
rolling air.

Find the grammar of resistance. The hope that persists as
you persist navigating heat, incontinent wind patterns, death
everywhere, the recycled repetition of nature.

Amplification of uncharted loss.

> From the blue way you envelop the world,
> the blue way you adore it.
> I'm saddened and in love with your blue way — with the
> blue way of presence in which you attend my readiness to
> live and die in this world.
> - Jaime Saenz, "The Immanent Visitor"

Here we imagine being in the apocalypse. We are already
there, approaching the beautiful and final end.

> We are living in the apocalypse. The first moment of time
> was the first moment of apocalypse and death. Please,
> don't fear the apocalypse.
> - László Krasznahorkai

Here it makes sense to linger, the slowness of the world that exists without you, how beautiful the world is in its indifference to my moving around in it, my idiotic and futile "pursuits" and "gestures" and "goals" and "things to do."

My rebellious angles only performances of impulses in that grand scheme of hysteric sturdiness. It exists, the world. As do I. But the paradox at the heart of this is that its indifference passes into me as a physical expression. I want to be anatomized by the landscape. I want to resemble more, a drifting dotted line that only fades away. Even the wind wraps itself around a body caring little what the body is, does, looks like.

In Bela Tarr's *Satantango*, everything seems to make perfect sense while watching an eight-minute-long shot of a slow moving herd of cows. The movement of cows through the mud as an action, to inhabit the weather in this way, to be inhabited by the rain: this is a privilege. The ability to feel content or elated or sad, as *privilege*.

The reticence of slowness is not a form of misery, but it is a form of suffering, of endurance. The mud and moo of history that stains our lungs is also what fills our intention with the will to move. Forward.

Dead fish everywhere.

I see what has been done, the verticality of past inside present, present inside past, and the flattened death of constructions. Dead hope in these buildings manifested now as sublime beauty. So they might be remembered. So they might be preserved. So they might mean something.

How to be reminded of the suffering of life if not through

the intense beauty of death.

The poetics of a space has to do with articulating the inarticulateable.

> To look at the end,
> the text without words,
> some words led toward it
> (almost to it),
> they came to a halt,
> no, they flagged
> in awful grief
> because of all that.
> - Ernst Meister, *In Time's Rift*

> Apparition is repetition of repetition, repetition's repetition. Then what could it possibly mean to say that a ghost returns for the first time if the ghost begins by coming back?
> – David Appelbaum, *Jacques Derrida's Ghost: A Conjuration*

The Salton Sea starts to embody a poetic form. For me: the sestina. Here the sestina is performed better as wordless words, its rules bent and the haunting quality of the repetition that defines the sestina as a form *felt*, the constant conjuring and reconjuring of ghosts, that uncanny feeling of déjà vu, that unmistakable quality of being haunted. *This* is the creation of the poem.

I think of Wilco's song "Jesus, etc." which Eileen Myles, in a poetry workshop I TAed, used as an example of the "quality" of the sestina. That is, the song doesn't follow the poetic scheme assigned to a sestina as a rigid form, but instead enacts a conjuration of the *feeling* of a sestina, those strange and irregular repetitions, reminders, ghosts, a magnetized compulsion of the *again*.

It is too much to assume sincerity, but in the falsified repetition of things, there is the interiorization of mourning that finds itself, finds *you*, and becomes a proclamation of truth.

The affect of form. The stitched-together fabric inundated with tears, then torn apart, then restitched together by flickering candlelight.

Douglas Kearney's poem "In the End, They Were Born on TV" enacts this uncanny anxiety too, induced by the possibility of repetition, the potential of it, the déjà vu, and the warped sensation of repeated lines that manifest like the vociferation of ghosts that phantomize the language and space of the page in a way that guarantees that the revenant of language's failure of precision will return and return again.

> people in their house on TV are ghosts haunting a house haunting houses.
> pregnant women in their houses on TV are haunted houses haunting a house haunting houses.
> our living room a set set for us ghosts to tell ghost stories on us.
>
> Would you be to-be on TV?
> To be the we we weren't to be and the we we're-to-be to be on TV.
> the pregnant woman agrees to being a haunted house haunting flickering houses. yes ok yeah yes.
> - Douglas Kearney, *Patter*

The Salton Sea's repetitions: fish, water, birds, sky, mountains, pink, blue, water, pink, bones, fish, bones, the heat, water...

Repetitions that sustain apparent separation from the wound.

You remember that you are wounded.

You remember that this might all be for *something* and self-ishness is already deeply embedded into the act of poetry.

The enactment of a haunting, a haunted place, a haunted body that reverts between the haunter and haunted.

I could write a sestina here, but the experience becomes the poem in this instance, or, perhaps, this articulation of thoughts and memories.

The remembering, the inability to remember, those moments that compose the poetics of this particular space. Whose space? Who ever occupies it for a series of moments, or lets the space occupy her?

The disclosure of the feelings a voyage brings on could take you hostage. None of these sentences can explicate *that* experience, but still, you are taken and ripped apart by such forces as the sun.

I write the following in my journal:

Here I confess that the sound of the fish bones crunching under my feet is so utterly satisfying, that the strange absence of the dead fish today (there hasn't been a die-off) is disappointing. Because there are no fish, I notice instead the dancing glints on the water, the red and yellow and golden glints and shimmers that jump and hop their way towards the shore, fading into the white foam or ebb into the light pink shore of bones. The strange quality of light that casts a surreal aura over the garbage that litters the beach, the rocks. The garbage almost looks beautiful here. This is my privilege to say so. A place of death, of sadness, of incredible beauty. I take off my sunglasses and it is so bright I can barely keep my eyes open. The mountains fade farther into the backdrop of the sky, the beyond. People are landscapes are changed are ruined. The sky is not blue, brackets us together, the disjunctions are fabricated within us, withered branches of trees, dry bones of fish, the layers of death are not just beneath our feet. I can not empathize with a dead fish. Familiarity is a weakness. No, it is persistence from one history to another. The pitch of my voice when I scream underwater, mottled.

The foam wall approaches.

MORNINGS IN BED

VLADIMIR: We are happy.
ESTRAGON: We are happy. (Silence.) What do we do now, now that we are happy?
VLADIMIR: Wait for Godot. (Estragon groans. Silence.) Things have changed here since yesterday.
ESTRAGON: And if he doesn't come?
VLADIMIR: (after a moment of bewilderment). We'll see when the time comes. (Pause.) I was saying that things have changed here since yesterday.
ESTRAGON: Everything oozes.
VLADIMIR: Look at the tree.
ESTRAGON: It's never the same pus from one second to the next.   — Samuel Beckett, *Waiting For Godot*

Do you remember what you wrote in the margins last night?

Stretch one trembling thigh, and then the other.

The whole fanciful inventory of a body.

The space of the morning.

What is it about waking up?

The space of one's own bed.

What is waking up an exit from? An entrance to?

Asleep. Awake.

Sleep as evidence of morality?

The secrecy of lapses.

This morning, the heart is heavy. Insanely heavy, like a brick inside my chest. The tears want to come so much but they do so sparingly. There are not enough tears for this heavy of a heart.

The sun is penetrating and the light is bright. A strange warmth wraps around my body but I feel cold, exposed. The air is permeated with an immense and beautiful melancholy and what I would give to be lying somewhere else right now. What I would give to linger here for a few moments longer.

This is the feeling of sitting up in bed, just slightly, not fully ready to get up, to leave the position of lying down, yet lingering for as long as possible in this in-between state, in this state—no matter what time it is—before the day begins. This is a motion, a physical gesture, a physical state in which the body lingers. Yet it is not a physical state at all. It is an emotional one. The lingering of my body, the physicality of this lingering becomes emotional, grave, persistent.

I think: I miss my mother.

I think: I miss another warm body in bed with me.

I think: I miss the safety of two warm bodies aligning and coordinating in gestures of passion and honesty.

Even in this state I can recognize the shameful sincerity of my situation. I do not miss *you* or even *you*. I miss the sensation of *you*. I miss the warmth, the questions. Ghosts that fulfill the duties of other ghosts. Expendable and petty impulses of arms, legs, fingers.

What about the bed becomes such a space of catastrophe, then peace, then catastrophe again? How is it that only inside an actual beating heart might a person find real peace?

I am currently living in a temporary space. So in this space, this temporary, weighted space, I lie in a bed that is not necessarily my own. This space, the bed, but also my psychological and emotional space, becomes a hollow but redeemable shroud: the simple comfort of warm sheets between your bare legs. The simple comfort of *another*.

In this space the bed is not so easily separated from the space of the room from the space of my heart from the space of the morning from the space of the sunlight sifting through the lacy white fabric covering the window.

I read words in a book and the space of the language in the novel becomes the space of my own strange and haunting relationships, resurfacing, repeating, renewing, becoming.

Are we having fun yet? – Michael J. Seidlinger

There are strange things to do in bed in the morning.

Lie in bed. Stare at the sunlight. Wonder what color is the sunlight coming in, what color is the light, what color.

The most suitable color for everything is the desire for color when is there too much of it. Having worked around dust, I can see the collections of dust around the edges of books, other objects, that melancholic border of dust that separates past from present, order from filth. Slivers of a room that remain untouched while the rest of it, the space that is, is parceled out in fragments of grief.

The dull, daily struggling of memory.

Repression closing down borders, permitting light and time and sin. An aiming toward. An aiming away.

Stretch out your limbs and *feel* because your emotions are heightened and you can *feel*.

Stretching —

Listen to the rain, if it is raining.

If it is raining, it is glorious. It is always a good time to hear the rain.

Listen to the music that generates those feelings only *that* music can. It is time. To have *those* feelings.

Notice the hawks circling in the sky outside. Open your eyes. Open yourself to every possibility in the universe, in your body.

The bed: in the morning, not having arisen, becomes a strange space for contemplation. The body: rested but not quite ready to move. The head: intimately still within another realm yet awake yet cloudy yet perceiving.

In bed, I have perhaps also broken my 10-month long writer's block. Since *Damnation*, I have not been able to write except on assignment and via collaboration. With *Damnation*, my relationship with language changed. So did my relationship with the world. Bela Tarr brought me out of an emotionally flat state and thrust me into one where I now feel like I am a vampire, equipped with this foreign yet familiar and heightened sense of everything.

Suddenly, I can *feel* everything. Everything is feel-able. Everything is a confession. Everything is uncertain. Everything is everywhere.

Reconstructed sleepless nights.

This or that presenting itself as a descent.

Attempts to wring feelings out of feelings.

Attempts to cry.

Lately I cry in bed often. I miss my mom. I miss all of the men I have ever loved, still love. I realize that I have a lot of love to give. I want so much to love. I do not mind the crying. It reminds me that there is no feeling like being in love and being loved back. There is no feeling like wanting to be in love, and wanting to be loved back. There is no feeling like heartbreak, like regret, like happiness, like sadness. All are feelings to savor. They linger, still, and I let them.

Lately too, I have been thinking about empathy, empathizing on an irregular level. A colleague brings up the term the "standardization of affect." I agree. Sympathy runs rampant. Affect has become standardized, moralized. Empathy seems harder and harder to formulate, but more and more *necessary*.

To me though, Nietzsche's famous Turin horse incident seems easier and easier to understand. It feels close. It feels like it is inside me.

The giddy horror of empathy.

An imperfect map towards closure, towards relief.

The Orphic lens of daring to go there, of understanding.

An impulse to look away. The impulse to keep looking.

In bed, I am watching TV. It is not morning, but night. I can not sleep. I am watching *Marvel's Agents of S.H.I.E.L.D.* It is late, maybe 3 in the morning, which could be considered night or morning. I haven't slept yet, and tonight I won't. The night and morning will blur together into a mass of gradually shining light that slowly grows outside my bedroom window. Morning will have come when I realize that I need to go to the bathroom to pee, notice what time it is, get "up."

The scene in *Marvel's Agents of S.H.I.E.L.D.* is simple. For your average viewer, it is the final scene of an episode that reveals some new information about a character assumed to be dead, ending the episode on a mysterious note. For me though, in that moment, I suddenly feel the impulse to respond to this scene, to go further. Is this a remnant of working through *Damnation*? Can I now only write when prompted to by an outside source? Film? Television? Joss Whedon? Regardless, the scene, that might be summarized very differently and much more succinctly by someone else, becomes articulated like this:

He wakes up out of a long and deep sleep. How long has he been sleeping? He can't remember— He can only remember— He feels his body aching. His face is burning and he smells the distinct smell of burnt flesh. He is seized by panic. He is in a strange bed. It might be morning, indicated by the yellow walls. He tried to get up slowly but it hurts to move and he can barely keep his eyes open. His eyes feel swollen, or like being torn apart. He removes the sheet covering his legs, looks down, sees a bandaged stump where his right leg used to be. He is confused. He moves his gaze up, calls out in hopes somebody might have some answers, in hopes this might be a dream, calls out again: *Hello? Anybody?* Maybe God is listening. Maybe he is being punished. He thinks briefly about his son. Maybe this is a dream. A horrible dream. He moves his gaze further up and sees a mirror on the opposite wall, sees himself vividly. It is his face. Worn, tattered, burnt, barely recognizable, but the essence of himself, the *him* that only he can recognize, the essence that one is oneself, the inarticulateable recognition of your own self that can not be simulated in a dream. It is there, it is *you*, you are here. And then, a flash across your vision, as if lasered across your retinas, *Good Morning Mr. Peterson.*

> No setting sun view for me, it is too melancholy; let me see him rise. – John Wilkes Booth to his sister, Asia

In a recent trip to the Mütter Museum in Philadelphia, there is a display of a fetus with exencephaly, a disorder in which the brain is located outside of the skull. The placard next to the display reads: *This condition is incompatible with life.*

Good morning.

TIDE POOLS & RAIN

Always bird.
Always water.
Always blue.
Always, listen.

The bird flies overhead, one bird, many birds.

The water is blue, isn't blue, is some color.

The blue is a color that I perceive, feel, touch, fades way into green, darkness, foam.

To be born in an instant, to listen, to huddle in the corner for the first time: cold.

To listen.

The water isn't blue.
It is *so* blue. All of it.

The sky meets the water. The sky, too, is not blue. And both are just as far away as *faraway*. That distance of unattainable and intangible. So much longing out there colored blue. Isn't. Is.

Indeed, it is. Blue.

Written:

To lean over perched on a rock lean over a little bit to be level with the water tides rushing inching towards your eyes the blue green foam making its way to that space right between your eyes to stand upright looking down to feel lightheaded from getting up too quickly the flies pesky the tide coming in quick around your ankles splashing upwards the feeling of jeans tight and wet against legs the sound of rushing rushing water the sounds the rushing the tide is coming in further the sun is bright and there are many pebbles and the sky is no other color but blue the blue blue sky it is bright the water glistens the roar of the waves the warmth of the sun the hours inside the wet puddles carved into stone and anemone beneath pebbles stories under rocks pelicans above and water and flies the shoreline doesn't end doesn't begin the blue isn't blue the water isn't blue the flatness of the sky against the moving water wavering tossing upended into against the sky it is loud it is loud can you hear?

Tide pools are giant spaces, shrunken down to fit. The rocks are humongous boulders on the backs of many beings like Sisyphus, worn down by time and patience and agony.

The ocean is eternity. What to write under the sun surrounded by rocks, by water? What to write?

Can you hear?

The recognition of sound.
The pleasure of it.
The affirmation.
The joy.

An internal diameter that widens to assume sincerity, to open up for ink-stained drips along the horizon line that separate blue from blue.

In Palos Verdes at the tide pools, it is blue and it isn't, and if I could embrace the sky, focus in on its illuminating and radiant manipulation like a confirmation of fleeting moments dancing like light-drops, I could reveal even one deliberate evocation of love and perhaps decrease this gap between us.

Always in parallel. Always an arrangement of the unseen.

Then, outside in the rain and thinking about the color blue.

It is raining and the rain makes my whiskey taste better.

Always rain.
Always glorious.
Always the sound.

The wind, too, that makes everything move, says my friend.
The wind that makes me feel a certain way, I say.

Because it moves, she says. Because of the wind, I say.

Here's the thing. One kind of pain isn't synonymous with
another. But one does draw a connecting line to another. I
think of heartbreak, of love. I think until the tears spill out
and mix willingly with the rain. I think of a touch, fingertips
along the small of my back, fingertips running parallel along
my spine to reach my shoulders, my neck, my face. I think,
fuck, I miss *that*. I *miss* that. I miss a feeling, a certain feeling,
a feeling of saying *I love you*. I miss saying *I love you more
than anything in the world*.

To miss feelings and the feelings of saying certain words.
Because words matter. Because words can never match the
complexity of what is felt but words are the only approxima-
tion we have.

Except when you hold my hand, run your fingers along my
fingers. Except when you look at me and pull me close. Ex-
cept, when everything else.

To miss the kind of discourse that happens between two

willing parties, the excess of it all, the necessity.

Dear G (who is no one now), I am glad to have known you.
I am glad to know that your tears only resemble lies and that
in the end you don't understand a single thing, not a thing at
all. Thanks though, for the heartbreak, perhaps the cruelest
and greatest gift of my life.

Differences marred and rapidly reset as water that falls from
gray clouds.

I am magnificently alone out here.

The goal is that the persistence to remember will become the
insistence to forget.

> Everything you say makes me want to die. I just told the
> biggest lie.
> - Elliot Smith

One pain into another. Heartbreak. The chilling wind. Grief.
The cold is glorious. The chill that reminds you of crystallized
sadness, precisely here that you incorporate yourself into the
kind of sadness that gives you relief. Swiftly, solicited tears
arrive.

Link one immediate past to another. Glimmers of your smile

What is it about Elliot Smith that makes me sadder than any
other music? Why am I addicted to that sadness?

I take off my glasses and the glistening glints off the wet
grass are magnified, blurred, stirred.

Here's the thing: I can't stop loving you.

Any of you.

Here's the thing, I'm not impervious to it but my presence is my willingness, is my iteration, is my stance.

This is my stance on it all within the frame of finitude.

Eventually things get still again.

In bed again, writing:

Crying because my hands are on my stomach warm and I'm remembering the comfortable embrace of last night the warmth of the sun coming through and he is still there and at that moment who he is doesn't matter just that he is there, that he is still there and it is morning and he doesn't have anywhere else he needs to be at that moment and turns to me to ask if I want coffee and that might be the most romantic gesture in months because that gesture is what I am thinking about right now crying in bed after a day at the tide pools and I can be transported to that latte from this morning and to that latte from Friday and to the latte with almond milk from last week the comforts of coffee the comforts of morning embraces of morning kisses of crying in that same bed that same bed where another him might have confessed his love for me but couldn't and this temporary love where I can feel the overwhelming love I have for all of them that love means heartbreak means love means tears means feeling means breathing means breath means the taste of scotch means the taste of beer on my tongue means his fingers gently caressing my leg means the feeling of my fingers on the pebble-covered sea anemone do you understand what that feels like? Life under those tiny pebbles the slime the moving the instability the softness the moving the gentle touch needed.

Do you see that it is the touch I need right now?

And I am not over it I am not
over anything.

But I persist.

There is a place that doesn't exist anymore.
I visited it yesterday in my sleep where I saw my mother
driving toward a fallen tree.
Go and watch.
The obligation of an imagination is to eventually smile.

LANDING SITES, HEAT, & AIR DENSITY

> Estragon: We came here yesterday.
> Vladmir: Ah no, there you're mistaken.
> Estragon: What did we do yesterday?
> Vladmir: What did we do yesterday?
> Estragon: Yes.
> — Samuel Becket, *Waiting For Godot*

Last week I was living with a few different books. I was rereading *Waiting For Godot* by Samuel Beckett and *The Stranger* by Albert Camus, two books that have affected me profoundly. Simultaneously I was dipping in and out of *Architectural Body* by Madeline Gins and Arakawa in preparation for a reading at LACMA last Saturday.

I was thinking about how to reconfigure and recast the way we exist in relation to space, the ways in which we see ourselves in these spaces recasted, the ways in which we reconfigure ourselves, the ways we try to understand this reconfiguring. This is perhaps a matter of consciousness or perception or architecture. But also emotion and empathy.

I hear the line: *All air is dense.*

I think: the words in these books aren't *felt* the same way heat is.

Lately, it is true that the air in this city has been dense, the embarrassed sun creating a strange sort of distance between bodies, mirages, and a magnetic reduction of space.

I can't deny the distance between us.

I can't deny the diabolical susceptibility of my heart either.

Even the shadows are receding.

Everything is mediated by words.

How anonymous is the distance that is texture. How tempting is it to touch everything? How is it that we resist?

In Los Angeles last week, it was devastatingly hot. Devastating is an overstatement, an exaggeration, if describing just the temperature outside. But it is not an overstatement if describing the feelings of a single body in a single week, a week that began with Mother's Day, an increasingly heavy, distant, and enclosed contingency. On this day, driving with a friend, we saw a reservoir covered in thousands of eerie, black, plastic balls. On another day, I watched *Godzilla*, empathized with a monster who was a participant in the demolition of entire cities. I watched *Volcano*, because I felt nostalgic, watched the destruction of an imaginary Los Angeles, witnessed a volcano emerge out of the La Brea tar bits, located right next door to LACMA where I read Saturday.

From *Architectural Body*:

> Similarly to how she flexes her muscles, a person flexes her surroundings—both are with her and of her always. Landing-site dispersal and a flexing of the circumambient determine and describe the world that lies within one's ambit of the moment. A person who is noting what is around her is dispersing landing sites; as body-wide landing-site dispersal registers the body's immersion within a volume held in place by certain demarcations, recording particulars about boundaries, a person will feel herself surrounded first according to one description of the world, then another. Moving within an architectural surround, a person fashions an evolving matrix, an architectural surround not entirely of her own making. Repeatedly, incessantly, a person surrounds herself by conforming in a particular set of ways to what surrounds her. Constrained by her environment, she proceeds to piece together an ar-

chitectural surround that maps onto the one within which she finds herself. In a glance, she takes in a tree, a lake, or a wall. Glancing in that direction again, but this time having lifted, for example, her right leg to start walking toward X, she ...

∞

Preexisting those who enter them, architectural surrounds stand as elaborately structured pretexts for action. Ready and waiting to be entered, even when in disarray, they are always encountered and often-noticed but little-understood atmospheric conditioners. Someone might make a convincing case for doubting that she exists or that isolated objects do, but it would be preposterous for her to try to use doubt to wipe away features and elements of an entire architectural surround. It would be unusual and unlikely for someone holding a glass beneath an open faucet and filling it with water to doubt the existence of either any part of this situation or of the situation as a whole. The question "Is this real or an illusion?" would seem not to be an option at such a moment. This whole situation— the sink, faucet, running stream of water, glass, hand, kitchen floor, wall-tiles, and windows, for a start—is of her sensorium within which she pours all liquids and drinks them up, but it is also constructed in place and is as such a place she can enter and with which she can link up in all manner of ways. All organisms-persons work hard, but none could work that hard, that is, no one could pull off the creation of an entire kitchen with water-producing faucet without prods, prompts, and props—that is, without the help of that set of features characteristic of this appliance-filled architectural surround. It would also be ridiculous for someone using a flashlight to find the path out of a labyrinthine cave and bumping up against uneven walls and low overhangs or tripping upon rocks and stalagmites and then sliding into and splashing through shallow puddles to wonder if indeed this might be a hollowed-out figment of her imagination.

In one space I become the sum of the heat and the objects in a room. In another, I can't remember where I just was.

I want to know how to just maintain the security of being, but of course, this is an impossibility. That kind of security is ever-elusive, ever-eager, ever-familiar, ever-after. Even the question of how to increase one's own human dignity, if it exists in the first place, and then, to simply trace rivers in the air with your fingers, concentrate on expanding, like the heat.

When the sun retreats, it feels the space it once illuminated become hollow. Is there singing? Dying wings of birds that fall from the sky. Huddled against the gathering dark, we tremble and wait.

In one moment the darkness is stillness, wretched nightmares of night. Where does the time go?

In another, relief. The falling of stars that resembles howling. The future drained through the moonlight. Moving silence.

I am silent in the space and then I give into the dead things beneath my feet. I wait to fall in love. Resist it. I am not ready. I am willing.

I repeat like a mantra: Nothing will ever break my heart again.

Dead tree: I know the mantra is a useless one.

Hesitation: Altered by sky.

So often the original seems to get lost and an inhabitation becomes an unlived one, or the production of that imaginary piece of knowledge that seems to connect everything together.

None of it is ever completely decidable.

Things just happen when we don't realize it.

Bodies become integrated into spaces without warning.

Last week, too, I followed the moon, the stars. Each night a different moon, each night a different sky, a different place, a different angle, a different space, a different—

The heat. The dusty sky. The fires. The heat. The color. Driving in the heat. The moon. Between the trees. Walking along a bridge where past suicides make it hard to breathe.

I found it hard to breathe.

Breathe.

Living with a book that completely describes the architecture of a week, and then again, not at all.

Living with so many feelings, charting the sky and attempting to understand what the sky looks like on different days, the sky as a consequence of a certain view of the sky as a consequence to a certain relationship with architecture.

My body aches from last night when I stood for moments with my head thrown back, attempting to glimpse the sky more fully, more bodily. How far am I right now from the center of the earth?

Today: the density of bodies.

Again: the density of air.

In the heat, it is hard to breathe, hard to think clearly, hard to articulate thoughts. In the heat, my relationship with language changes. The words melt like Dali's clocks, I intend, try to remember intention, and instead feel a heavy feeling in my chest. The heaviness replaces the words and my mind goes blank, my mind only filled with hot gas, my heart: heavy, and I think: *I want there to be more space around things*, and I think: *No, I want there to be no more space between things. Between us.*

Bodies: touching.

We talk about your aversion to talking about feelings. *It makes me feel weird*, you say. *It makes me feel like I'm peeling my skin off.*

I think about my desire for words and language and words and language *about* feelings. *What about gestures and actions?* You say. I can't think of a good response. Indeed, what about them?

There is a persistence in feeling. Persistence in feeling as time as weight as sunlight as heat as the fires that burn and change the color of the sky.

Imagine: to light a match and to change the color of the entire sky.

In this instance, I feel like I am unable to be honest. I want to desire something and to be able to take it, to not care about anything but my own happiness. What makes me happy?

Sometimes the answer is easy. Sometimes it is intermittent, hidden, rare, like the rain, or the communiques from a person that only knows now how to write words. Meaningless words. Words are so meaningless, aren't they?

I think I must be waiting for something, or delaying the kind of response someone thinks they might deserve. The truth is, so much of these relationships come down to words, to semantics, to language.

But beneath all the language, there are feelings. Imprecise, incorrect, permeable, malleable feelings.

And for the first time, in a long time, the words start to mean *something*.

BACKPACKING, POINT REYES, DRIVING

Recently memory fails. Recently, memory is failing.

In different places, different proximities and distances from home, memory wavers.

This past weekend I went backpacking with my brother in Point Reyes National Seashore in Marin County. This is a place that resonates a certain calm and unsilent quietude. The gift of giving oneself over to a territorial time and space. Of creating distance between yourself and the city.

A friend tells me, in no exaggerated manner, that sometimes you just need to be near the trees.

Somewhere and sometime when the traces of something beyond become more than just the residue on my boots, but an entirely spatial and real environment to *be* in.

In the incredibly lush and green and dense space of the woods, daydreaming trees, organic substance, reverie of forgetfulness when surrounded by dragging memories and roots, I utter different words, pieces of language, to myself in silence. As my body continues to move, feet treading ground, walking forward, I start to think of the poetic form as a *stance*.

The sestina, as a form, tends to conjure and reconjure ghosts, the uncanny repetition that induces haunting, déjà vu, strange warpings and relocations of memory.

Echolocation.

So the way my eyes wrap around the tree, wrap and rewrap around the trunk, the branches, my eyes darting between leaves and green and trunk and moss and sky and leaves and dirt and green and green again, this uncanny experience of the tree might be one stance, say, a sestina.

But a different stance, one in which I step back to observe the tree as an isolated and outlined object, the one tree sitting among many, the outline of green in the context of a backdrop that serves to spotlight *this* tree, *the* tree. Perhaps, this might be a haiku.

Or another stance altogether. Perhaps, as the sun sets, and the colors that the setting suns creates through its alter ego of time and wonder, the altered saturation of greens and oranges and purples and the shadows that are now cast on and from the tree, a strange illumination of something majestic, royal, yet sad, loyal, and fixed. This, perhaps, is a sonnet.

Or the lurking group of quails that congregate around an empty camp site, scurrying down the path just ahead of me, unafraid, beckoning or mocking or completely apathetic to whatever it is I am doing, their sounds and intimate collaboration with the tree. Here now, a pantoum?

And then, out here, there is too the simultaneity. On the way up to the camp site, a 4.6 mile hike with our backpacks, we see a deer on the path in front of us. He is unafraid. In fact, he approaches us. He approaches so closely that he circles the perimeter and as I get out my phone to take a picture, he stops for a full moment to look at me, as if posing for the camera, before skipping and disappearing into the green backdrop. As I think about the beauty of the moment, I am plagued simultaneously with Louis CK's voice in the background, his bit on the stupidity and audacity of deer, his anecdote of the deer, that he claims, actually ran *into* his car. Out here, all memories and stories and myths are simultaneous.

Lately, it is as if all my senses have been heightened. In *The Vampire Diaries*, and in countless other pop culture vampire mythologies, one of the side-effects of being a vampire is the heightened sense of everything. The heightened sense of touch, emotion, feeling, sensation, love. The wind feels more intense as it passes across your skin. Anger is intensified. The sex is more passionate. Etc. In general, one *feels* more. Is this possible? Or does it become a matter of perspective? Of what gets noticed or unnoticed in each perceived moment of each perceived existence?

From my particular point of view at this very moment in time, I look back and see my life divided up into three periods. First, the period before my mother's death: a past that is difficult to remember, almost a daydream, figments of another life with mountain ranges that separate my current self from all else that dwells back there. Then, a period of flatness and depression: utterly content and comfortable yet without happiness or joy. Then a period after an intense heartbreak. The details are extraneous. What matters is that I have trouble remembering anything from past periods in my life. As if they happened in other lifetimes, or not at all.

Inversion of images. There is enough room for you here but I'm not sure if I want you here yet, with me.

There is something I want to say about Pasolini and the long take here. But I can't quite remember.

Triggers for memories now can come in the form of a hawk circling overhead or a song lyric on the radio. Triggers for memories now may no longer trigger memories but stories and myths.

While driving back to Los Angeles, moving forward in my car, I am thinking. That sounds simple. I'm thinking in the car. But I get some of my best thinking done in the car. Every single detail that I pass through becomes a potential trigger for a memory or a thought.

That crevice on the rock: the feeling of being small.

That field of wheat: the pleasure of pretend labor in a video game.

That sky: the memory of loving someone and wanting to die.

That black crow swooping down: a glimmer of intense and dulling pain.

Trust me when I say that the impulse to observe and feel everything is overwhelming.

Trust me when I say that the impulse to observe and feel everything is also compulsory.

Trust me when I say that my relationship to language has changed completely and when I say I don't see the world anymore I mean that I see everything and the entire world and it is blinding.

In *Damnation* I started to write about the preciseness of language and the momentum of sentences in a way that I hadn't cared about before.

Now, it feels like there aren't enough words for anything. That language, which always and inevitably fails yes, seems even more inadequate to describe *anything*, *any* feeling, *any* experience.

I don't know how to write anymore. Or I don't know how to pick out the words from the vicarious cloud of profession that is constantly circling around like locusts.

Sitting silently in a space, this space or that space, or another space, I am feeling something that I have never felt before. This is felt partially via the silence of the space, or at least the silence of myself, the silence that occurs because I can not and will not find words to describe this space. Instead, the moment of the space becomes a silent utterance, felt inside my own body only, an encounter that happens once and to never happen again, a stance that constantly adjusts itself, wanting to become a poem perhaps, but as yet too over-whelmed to try and find the words.

Where are the words?

Today, I am speechless.

I am increasingly speechless. Or wordless. Or—

Let's just say that I don't know how to handle words the way I used to. Or, they don't handle me the way they used to.

Tossed back, from one wall to the opposite wall.

In order to speak of daydreams, one needs to be able to leave this world first.

In order to go on an excursion, one needs to be reminded how imagination antedates memory and how distance is necessary and fierce.

Trust me when I say that I no longer fear death.

I'm composing this piece in the car while driving back to LA. I'm composing this in the car while speeding down the highway, my eyes trying to focus on the road but instead darting frantically around me watching the sky, the clouds, the quickly changing landscape, my eyes moving between outside and touchscreen.

Yes, scold me. Absolutely. This is a dangerous and irresponsible action. I agree.

Yet I am compelled to continue. In the space of the car, a strange space that exists in the context of a much more open space. An open road, an open landscape, this California that speeds by outside my windows, as I move through it all in this confined vehicle which is closed and restricted yet I feel the movement and I feel the air and I feel the breath and I feel the speed and I feel the sadness and I feel the joy and I feel that there is someone that I miss very much and am I speeding to see them or am I simply traveling at a speed that has been dictated by the blue, blue sky.

THE SALTON SEA II

> The spiritual life, to which art belongs and of which she is one of the mightiest elements, is a complicated but definite and easily definable movement forwards and upwards. This movement is the movement of experience. It may take different forms, but it holds at bottom to the same inner thought and purpose.
> — Wassily Kandinsky, *Concerning the Spiritual in Art*

Sometimes one wonders what it means to breathe rather than to utter a sound, to blow air rather than blow music. The difference between air and sound and breath.

Sometimes, the hardest part of creating art, is the complicated movement of experience. That is, my experience moving through the movement of a piece. Each day I walk through a certain space. History is silent while I walk, but my memories creep up in stages. It feels some days that I am walking for longer or shorter periods of time.

The landscape each day is different, is different each moment.

Each evening the sunset blows me away, differently, quietly, briefly.

The sunset is beautiful because it is ephemeral.

The impossibility of capturing the sunset in a work of art: the colors, the changing colors, the light, the clouds, the shadows, the residue of death and of life, the hope, the density, the lightness, the brevity of the moment, the fixedness, the impulses, the attachment, the compulsion, time changing direction.

What gets imprinted.

The wound of expectation.

The realm of assumption and the shades outside, lined up and blurring together.

Falling rain and letters.

Kandsinky resonates with me in such a way that perhaps he is describing my own inner landscape. The way it feels that in a certain quality of light different questions are asked between the particles of dust that float upwards and downwards.

> The solitary visionaries are despised or regarded as abnormal and eccentric. Those who are not wrapped in lethargy and who feel vague longings for spiritual life and knowledge and progress, cry in harsh chorus, without any to comfort them. The night of the spirit falls more and more darkly. Deeper becomes the misery of these blind and terrified guides, and their followers, tormented and unnerved by fear and doubt, prefer to this gradual darkening the final sudden leap into the blackness.

> At such a time art ministers to lower needs, and is used for material ends. She seeks her substance in hard realities because she knows of nothing nobler... The artist in such times has no need to say much, but only to be notorious for some small originality and consequently lauded by a small group of patrons and connoisseurs (which incidentally is also a very profitable business for him)...

> But despite all this confusion, this chaos, this wild hunt for notoriety, the spiritual triangle, slowly but surely, with irresistible strength, moves onwards and upwards.

At times an extremely minimal space, that is, a space split from the whole, a corner lit by a candle, a piece of sky with a particular cloud, a sad memory under the overpass, or simply one's face in the bathroom mirror, dreams emerge that reveal something completely different about a particular *fact* or *event*. The proximity to this *fact* or *event* within this space exacerbates a sort of communion. It becomes very, very dark. The thickness of the air, the silence. Hardly anything is bearable. It becomes light again though, as if darkness does not exist momentarily, so that you miss the darkness oh so much, so that things appear so differently now, having seen them in complete darkness and then in complete illumination.

Will Alexander and I often talk about how sometimes we feel like we are the only two left in the world who feel a particular way. I couldn't describe what it is we feel and think because there, in the need for description, is where the spiritual wall exists. But he often says something similar to this, in Kandinsky's words:

> The spirit, like the body, can be strengthened and developed by frequent exercise. Just as the body, if neglected, grows weaker and finally impotent, so the spirit perishes if untended. And for this reason it is necessary for the artist to know the starting point for the exercise of his spirit.

I used to wait until I was *free* or *had time* before embarking on any day trip as a sort of reward or respite from the quotidian drudgery of life. Now I wait until I am most overwhelmed, stressed, busy, when the lack of time is at its peak. Because it is *then* that I need a change of air the most. When I need to touch something else and lie down to look at the sky from a different set of coordinates.

I visit the Salton Sea for the second time this year, and this time, my mind is lingering with the question of *how to write a space*.

How does one write a space? How does one enter a space so fully, or ask the reader to enter the text as to experience the experience of a space? The movement of a space? All of the consequences, beautiful and horrible, of *being* in a space?

Distant and lean.

Nothing but a stone on the road.

Withdraw your hand.

To write the Salton Sea there are an infinite number of factors to consider:

The colors.

As if in an Impressionist painting. As if having died and come back to life again. As if in a daze and unable to fully open one's eyes. As if the colors are so diluted they run together but simultaneously are so vibrantly dull, so hideously pastel, so beautifully in-between states that all words for color become lost and drown there in front of you in the sea. Pinks, blues, browns, yellows, whites, greens. The saturation of the blue-blue water with the dulled pink-pink sky. Colors to vex eyelids, colors to drink and die in.

The textures.

The crackling of the fish bones below one's shoes. It's a natural compulsion to want to walk in and over them forever. It's a natural compulsion to want to lie in them. To feel the textures of the bones against your skin. The strange smoothness of the water. The jagged spines of the rocks. The correlation of texture to skin to sky to water to heat to skin to time. It happens that you slip and let yourself fall, grab a hold of a rock, feel the persistence of the pendulum of time as you take a handful of bones and dirt and sediment and let them fall between your fingers.

The air.

The quality of it. The immortal and instant deathly feel of
breathing, as if swallowing the forms of the fish, the ruins,
the purpose of it all. You have no choice but to breathe as
the space as no choice but to exist. All breath, again, woven.
All breath, here, as new. As you don't intend to escape. As
dragging and fog and filled mouthes.

The heat.

The Salton Sea and its surrounding areas, there's something
about being here in the summer. The density of the dry heat
that rubs you everywhere, that makes your eyes water, that
adds to the affliction of a place that only knows generosity
through death, that only knows love through eternal passion,
that only knows life through extinction, that only knows love
through color. You drink water like you drink to live. The
heat does that to you. You think you see things in the dirt, in
the shadows. This too is the heat, that you want to escape, yet
have the urge to linger in a little while longer.

The smell.

In some cases, it is possible to smell death, then, to continue
being calm, to continue one's good mood. Foul smells are
not always nauseating. They can move into that spectrum of
refreshing, that is, to be reminded of what death smells like is
to be reminded of how to breathe again.

The sky.

The sky looks different wherever you are. This too is the quality of light, which is absolutely distinct from the light in Los Angeles, for example. The inscrutable light moves through the space like a subsiding threshold of swiftness and color. An impossible task might be to map the movement of light through a space. One sees everything in a different light. What is offered, given. What is seen in the previous moment. That the sky is *there* and has a past, but its past is blue and therefore inaccessible.

Writing a space is about *feeling*.

It's about the intersection of one's intention and patience and existence with another's colorblindness and absence and languid imagination. It's about trying and failing. It's about, then, life and death, about attempting and arriving. Writing a space is about failure.

This probably isn't what you meant.

We should talk.

Of course.

There is the sense of serenity but also the exposure of one's purpose. The space knows *why* even before you do.

There are the ghosts. That is, each and every memory has followed you here, and therefore, all of your dead. You linger in a spot for longer than the moment really allows, fidelity to time as tantrum or forgotten, and as you feel the heat and the air and you smell the salty death on your tongue, the sweat pouring down your face, you feel a ghost whispering behind your ear, that revenant of the undecidable, the unknowable.

Depicting a fury that didn't exist before because the space

endows it now.

Depicting a grief that comes and goes more quickly than a famished wolf.

In a way, all spaces are haunted.

In a way, all spaces are about memory.

To sit in a space and feel and think and reflect and remember.

To remember.

To see what is imagined differently.

Really, to see.

Writing a space is also about honesty.

Last night while watching the latest episode of *Penny Dreadful*, there is a conversation between Ethan Chandler and Dorian Gray. Ethan Chandler remarks on seeing some very old Native-American paintings of animals. When asked why he likes them, he responds, "They're primitive. No. They're honest." They then discuss whether it is possible for modern art to be honest, and Dorian Gray says that at least in music, it is. *Because music is ephemeral. Music is phantasm.*

There is a question of honesty and wholeness when writing a space.

The Salton Sea, as a space, perhaps forces this. How else to operate when nothing is as it seems? When every moment must require so much intention in the thickness of the heat?

When your eyes don't work the way they do anywhere else and the memories you've brought with you become distorted and reimagined here?

The poetics of a space already dictate the poetics of a poem, a piece of writing, but sometimes we want to willingly ignore what the space has already written. There are less choices to make than it seems.

Moving pieces of thread and dust through the air. The movement of water. A single step forward. The memory. Perhaps, I do remember.

Hesitating I picture a dark entrance in the water in front of me, the landscape that is serene and clear. Upon my vision I draw a line to morsel out the colors into pieces. I am famished like the wolf, a bony frame and desire hanging out in the form of a tongue, dry and feverish and red. I have tried to be impartial but I have thought at length about the kind of concealment this space can provide. I imagine I am investigating my past, opening it up, but the vulnerability is not about exposure but the easy and convenient concealment of pain under sand and blue and death. The stench even allows me to withdraw into wretched beauty, and this protected space, lie the bony carapace of a Galapagos tortoise, spins words like golden strings and this dramatic incident of hunger pushes other memories to bubble up into that accessibly pool of *fact*. I remember now. The hesitation. I remember too that you are with me, and all the cast-offs from my previous atrophic scenes designate themselves into more digestible morsel.

Run my fingers through the sand again. Feel the heat. Close my eyes for a moment and then open them to see you standing over there a small distance away. Let an immense sadness sit inside my flesh a moment longer and attempt to find the origin of this dream. Then, remember.

In spite of poetic exaggeration, we are better when we are not alone.

Far off, I hear the whirring and monotony of the names of the dead being read from a very long list.

I am puzzled acutely by the accusation, but I confess that we are all guilty of something.

It doesn't have to be a word.

Oh, but it does, doesn't it?

OCEAN BEACH PIER

There it was, under the blue sky, the birth and death of mother.
It was mother's ghost, bearing the rain, who came to speak of
sorrow.
When one does not know to abandon her children, she does not
know the embrace of death.
Haunting isn't for the dead but for the living, be prepared for
the sea to be your confession.
Still, almost fearlessly, she stood there. Mother.

I recall something that Will Alexander says during dinner.
We're talking about the state of the world, about cosmic
energy, about the apocalypse, about everything that is already
here, about boxes, and about the weather. We discuss all the
things that writing seems to be *about* these days, how petty
some of these things seem to be. He remarks about how it's
petty to write simply about love affairs, for example. That
the only thing writing can be about now is weather, not love
affairs. Or love affairs *through* the weather.

I think about the rain and the heat and that indeed, nothing
seems more important than the weather. That, even with ev-
erything that is happening, it is the weather that will outlive
us or destroy us.

I think about the howling state of the world. Don't things
seems more chaotic than usual? Don't things seem calmer?
More serene? Doesn't it all feel a bit haunted to you?

I mean, I don't see how we can live in the same world and
I can feel all of these things and you can't. Where do our
worlds overlap these days? I feel increasingly distanced from
you and I'm not sure what this means.

Ocean Beach Pier at night, recalls a certain image. I always
remember one particular night when it was red tide and

so the incoming tides and subtle movements of the water revealed a strange and eerie glow, the small but numerous bioluminescent dinoflagellates causing the water to glow blue. The same night the pier was full of people fishing, different colored glow sticks tied to the ends of their lines for visibility. And amidst the already eerie symphony of light and darkness, the fireworks from Sea World started to go off. *I'm somewhere else*, I thought. It was utterly chaotic: all of the different lights and people and flopping fish and voices and boom boxes, and it was utterly beautiful and calm: the darkness, the glow, the perfect home for ghosts and their sorrow.

I talk with a friend about our *special places*. Those places that we go to for relief or inspiration or serenity or a break from everything else. That it is significant when you bring another person to one of those special places with you for the first time.

I bring you here and I hold your hand. I wonder what you are thinking about.

I wonder if you can hear the howling.

Of course, too, the Ocean Beach Pier holds a certain significance only in my imagination. It is *that* night I always recall when walking down to the edge of the Earth. It is *those* ghosts that I feel I can hear, even with the crying children and the smell of fish attempting to pollute my intimate moment with the sea.

When mother spoke out loud, the first word was blue.
Blue was the color of a confession given under the sign of the fish.
Swimming wildly under golden glints of sunlight, the fish only knew to embrace the sorrow.
Sorrow is mother is the utterance of a embrace that is the color blue.

Can't you feel it with your eyes, the intensity of its sorrow?
Only when you encounter death and its embrace can you feel the
sun setting behind your eyes.

At the end of the pier, it is like I am standing at the end of
the world. Standing on the southern tip, there is only dark-
ness and infinity and black and tiny hovering stars. If I stand
in the right position, the lights of the city don't even exist
anymore and I can consider the pain of infinite time. Frankly,
fear is relieving and only God knows what it all means but
it isn't difficult to simply turn around and be back in that
parallel reality again.

This is the ocean that can swallow you whole without flinch-
ing, without anyone noticing. You could disappear into the
blackness, and here, no one would ever notice. Is this a simi-
lar kind of loneliness to the terrifying solitude of outer space?

Dust and dust and dust of being. Of darkness. The kind of
black that swallows intimacy and charges one with cruel
indifference.

You have confessed to me that your greatest fear is being
alone.

I wonder why we are allowed to live.

Don't you realize that it's all always leading up to this one
moment of death.
Here the caw or beckon of a bird, here a creature's wound.
The wound is the only language that is understood by mother.
Glory is the sun is the fish's stomach embracing the eyes of death.
Or the sorrow is only known when death is a ghost behind your

shoulder, that blue embrace.
Feel with your eyes, and death might already exist at the bottom of your stomach.
I told you already, that it would be easy to change, if not for the wound of blue.

Today, the sun hasn't yet set. It is that in-between time.
Bare-footed regulars selling their wares alongside the shore.
One plays a flute with his nostril. Families are fishing. Kids
are running around without care for the couples who are
trying to stroll leisurely on a romantic evening out. I have the
urge to kick the kids, each and every one of them. Instead
I grab your hand and squeeze. I'm feeling very conflicted.
Some families have set up tents and radios. They will be here
for awhile.

The water is utterly blue and large patches of kelp decorate
the surface. The smell of fish is unmistakable, unavoidable. I
want to lean harder against the railings but they are covered
in bird poop and fish guts. I don't really care but I feel that it
would disturb you to see my arms covered in grime.

Today too, there is a visitor. A sea lion hovers beneath us like
a dog at the dinner table. He is enthusiastic, determined. He
does not leave. He starts to bark louder even. Louder.

Even with all of the people, it is incredibly calm to be here,
so close to the edge of the world, so close to infinity, so close
to dying. Like walking out to meet yourself. It is only *you* out
there, no one else.

Embracing the blue death of mother brings the rain, the night, the feelings.
Embracing mother brings the sorrow, the sky, the wound of confession.

I confess that I miss my mother.
Go, little bird, to the blue wound in the sky.
Go, taste the death of night and the color of salt: ghostly.
Ghosts that flutter like salt in the blue waves that beckon.
Ghosts that flutter between the blades of grass and call out
mother in the night.
It is night now and I can not sleep.
It is night now and I can sense the nostalgia of rain but the rain
is not here, no, not yet, the rain.
Mother, where are you?

There is, for me, a profound difference between the ocean
and the beach. I don't consider myself a beach person at all.
But the ocean is a wholly different place, a place where you
can confront the terror of loneliness, of the unknown, of the
deep, blue ocean that is the ocean.

The sun setting behind the clouds create radiant rays of light
that burst outwards like the cover of a religious pamphlet.
These are the kinds of scenes that can be used to justify the
existence of God, the kind of beauty that can be described as
holy, sacred.

Here it was, the extracted embrace of a cow's stomach lying out
there in the night.
Here it was, the salt of sorrow in the blue wound we call home,
the home that will soon be obliterated by the color of feeling, the
ghost of blue.
The home that will be covered over with your confession, a
dying fish out in the sun, neglected, haunted.
The cow is the fish set out to dry.
The cow is the stomach that churns during the sky's clear and
resonant confession.

The heat is what you feel when you wake up in the morning.
The heat of a million dying fish. It is night. It is blue.
Where is mother now?
Bring the light, says the dying fish.
It is already here, says the dead cow.
You are ghosts already, sings the sky, blue and salty and hidden
under your wound.
The ghost is what you feel when you wake up in the morning.

SPACES IN TRANSITION

The mornings in bed when you turn over to see someone there, a sleeping body you barely recognize. *Who is this person lying next to you and what is this overwhelming feeling you have?* For a moment you don't recognize this person who has somehow managed to infiltrate your life so seamlessly. Three months ago they didn't even exist. Today, they have taken over everything, become everything, are everything.

One moment, you feel you're in love. You've managed to fall in love. With a person. With *this* person.

Another moment, you genuinely think, *Who the fuck is this person? How did they get here?*

Palpable denial.

Or, a sadder prophecy.

Love is a perpetual space for transition. The spaces change and follow.

And everything rearranges around you, bristling.

Summer is not a season but a lingering shadow.

Summer is not a period but a burden of heat.

Summer is not summer but another space for dying.

In the heat, it feels as if I'm dying.

The hikes out under an afternoon sun. The sun is hazy and the green of the trees seems stranger, *greener* somehow. It is hot and the sweat won't stop pouring down over my brow, my nose, building up under my sunglasses. This is a place that once meant one thing and now means another. This is a place that depends almost entirely on the weather. The creek is almost nonexistent. The destination is a waterfall that is now barely a trickle. The sun is moving up there, and too, the moon is visible, like a transparent, crescent cloud that lingers like a spectral shadow.

The sun.

Again: the sun.

The steps outside in the middle of the night. You can't sleep because your head is full and your heart is heavy. Whiskey calms the nerves. Or heightens them. One or the other, but frankly the scooped stillness of the sky is still audible. You're sitting outside and it is cool and it is calm and your eyes are welling up with tears and you just want to lie down and sprawl across the sidewalk.

There is no sign of rain. It feels like it may never rain again.

You miss the rain.

You can't remember what it feels like.

You remember the *feeling* of rain.

You haven't cried in awhile. But you're crying now.

The "people out there" that don't seem to notice that the world is ending. That the end days aren't a distant future. There will be no quick and brutal end, not biblical, not disastrous, not immediate, not far away, but here and now and slow and gradual and present and now and now and today and this moment: dying. The weather tells us. The sky tells us. The ground tells us. The sun tells us. We are living in the apocalypse and the apocalypse is living in us now.

Dying is a synonym for living is a synonym for dying is a synonym for changing is a synonym for time.

Hope is light is fire is death.

Waiting is hope is eternity is sadness is feeling is death.

Love is happiness is living is memory is touch is beating is breathing is breathing is breathing is death.

The heart that remains in denial and can't reconcile the sludge pile of memories and emotions. *Why are feelings so complicated? So persistent? Such feelings.* Let's imagine that you can act on your feelings. That the feelings *matter* and can be acted upon. Let us *imagine.*

I am reminded of the desire to push you off a cliff. But I can't exactly remember why?

Part of me hates the silence, your silence.

But too, I can't deny the security of this feeling. The terror of it. Claws scratching at my throat from the inside.

The sky is different every day. The sky is not blue. The sky, in fact, is not always the sky.

The city is different each moment. This city is breathing and changing and living and dying and chanting a different prayer each morning, each night, each time the sun sets.

You are different each moment, seasons and faces that awake

at different densities of fog.

What can you remember about yesterday? What can you remember about the sun?

The clouds have gathered into a dense mass over there.

Over *there* is not over *here*.

I miss you already. How did this happen?

When you're walking around out there, don't you feel it? That intensity? That strange ringing in your ears, the eerie but momentary silence that signals *something is about to happen*.

Something has already happened.

NIGHT OCEAN

One must be receptive, receptive to the image at the moment it appears.
– Gaston Bachelard, *The Poetics of Space*

In one space the safety and cleanliness of a structured space, in another, the threat of extinction.

It is night, and it is dark, and always, faced with the vastness of an ocean that is black and moving and roaring, the threat of extinction, of utter annihilation. Yours. His. Everyone's.

The placid expressions of late-night joggers seem almost completely irrelevant next to that blackness that could swallow you whole. This is the closest to infinity you can get out here. Stains on the night. Surpassing.

How else can I say "I ever—"

Am I looking for death in all of these spaces?

What approaches over the water?

What the darkness conjures is an oath, the last and final breath, an expiration, that comes again and again with every roar of the tide coming in, with every absence of sight (you can't see anything in this light, it is blurry, the different darknesses run together, the horizon line a thick black border: phantom, ambiguous, wandering). The dilemma of sight requires the ghosting of memory, the water a translation of *water*, the darkness a distortion of *ocean*. What is exposed in the air? It is cold. One hardly has the opportunity to feel cold anymore.

Finding death.

Thundering sounds.

We walk slowly across the sand, light spreading.
We walk slowly across the water, light spreading.
We walk slowly across the sky, light spreading.

Can you grasp the simple feeling of empathy out here? That is, it's now impossible to feel empathy for anything. The disappearance of empathy as looming and imminent and dangerous as the catastrophic event that is yet to tear the planet apart. The planet *will* be torn apart. Can't you feel it coming?

The *feeling* of a ringing in my ears before an explosion, before something that is about to happen.

> Poetry is a soul inaugurating a form.
> — Pierre-Jean Jouve

What of the form if darkness? What of the form if a formless form, an ocean? What of resonance? Of temperature? Of being in love with your back against the rest of the entire planet on the other side of that blackening black under that strangely deep, profoundly blue sky. The darkest blue night.

The moon thinks it's hiding, exposed again, shifting lights.

That we can call such a breathless and formless thing a word: *ocean*. That we can hold these fixed memories of vertigo, moving lights, faces, all recalled by the sound of the water, the birds running along the shoreline, a handful of sand to feel the beach as a concrete thing. The feeling of sand is cold and expected. The feeling of loss, the breath that comes when you let the grains drop, and the arms that wrap themselves around you afterward, unexpected tremblings of moments.

I take steps towards one of the three birds. It refuses to fly, runs quickly over to the right.

So I waver towards the right, take a few steps toward another bird.

You ask me: *Why are you separating them?*

I don't know. I have no intention in mind.

In response to the perceived continuity of black ocean, I make a gesture filled with uncertainty and regret. Indeed, why?

Seek out the silence that makes your ears ring.

> At times, the simpler the image, the vaster the dream.
>
> We want to see and yet we are afraid to see. This is the perceptible threshold of all knowledge, the threshold upon which interest wavers, falters, then returns.
> – Gaston Bachelard, *The Poetics of Space*

The recognition that the end is very near. It is your responsibility. The guilt, the wound, the future.

Future wound guilt is a conjuration is a *towards* gesture, illegible but audible, inherited, present, the smell of archived lies and salt.

I'll come to you in the morning, the message of water.

I'll come again or I will be there already and I'll pass through each of the phantoms already circling, circling, sand and broken glass in my hand.

The ocean will speak when there is silence. There will be silence when we stop screaming. We will not stop screaming until we are all already dead.

Apocalypse no longer means the end days no longer means something to-come. It is the way of life, the expression of a permanently muted voice, the abundance of a certain quality of light, meditating under the moon, the inability to capture anything in an image.

We walk slowly across the sand, arms meeting.
We walk slowly across the sand, light meeting.
We walk slowly across the sand, hands meeting.

The gift that you cannot capture the image. The memory becomes the copy becomes the whisper becomes the oath.

I am honest when I say, *I love you.*

I am honest when I say, *I am terrified.*

I am honest when I say, *I don't understand any of this. You.*

The ocean is terrifying and it may swallow me whole, drowning in water or limbs torn apart by a bracketing of excess, but I am more terrified of my love for you. I don't understand where it comes from.

Do you understand that when the answers to your questions are, *I don't know*, it's not for lack of enthusiasm or decisiveness, it is the perceived trauma of some dark light that may enter at any minute. This is my crisis, not yours. It is my issue and failure, not yours. When I say, *I love you* and *I don't know*, these statements in the same sentence, same breath, same expression of oblivion, this is the most honest I can be.

We are all fated for failure.

But that failure can be caressed with the patient strokes of the blue waves and we can hold hands under the moonlight and draw swirls in the sky with our fingers to manipulate the clouds. We can fall together, and when they finally tear me away from you, I will not scream.

DEAD CALM

Perhaps the most important thing is that the sky isn't blue.

That is, once you recognize the sky as blue, you've lost something essential.

Once you acknowledge it, you can't go back. You can't *unsee* blue.

Let's recognize that when we're in a space, any space, that that space becomes a metaphor for humanness.

That humanness often has nothing to do with us and what we know and what we've done, but our failures, our feelings, our insistence to hold on to certain apparitions of the past that prevent us from truly moving forward.

That humanness often has to do with time itself, the waiting, the refusal to backtrack but the catatonic attacks of memory that protract certain moments, extend them, exaggerate them, like instances of forgery that become truth that become recollection that become presence.

Even in the laundromat, when the dignifying and distinguishing gesture is solely of waiting.

In the waiting, there is a chaos of possibilities, revelatory possibilities of the sun shining down, vertically, dialectics of what is indispensable and what is cursory. In the waiting, there is the sitting, there is the swirl of your underwear in the dryer, there is the eternal circular action of machines, there is the hum and the televisions, there is the constant return to boredom. Or, in this waiting, boredom is completely irrelevant. This is a heavier moment, one that is a relief and a burden. This waiting becomes a kind of slow indifference becomes a generous gesture on behalf of the universe. You can wait *here*. You *can*.

> We cannot identify ourselves with their feelings. But
> we enter into something more essential, into the very
> duration at the heart of which things penetrate and affect
> them, the suffering of repetition, the sense of another life,
> the dignity assumed in order to pursue the dream of this
> other life, and to bear the deception of this dream.
> — Jacques Ranciere

The waiting is not the gesture, but your interest in the waiting. The space in which you wait, i.e. the laundromat, a space for repetition for tedium for facility for reflection for confession for death. In waiting, you are waiting for death, and in waiting for death, you agree to keep living.

The feeling of waiting for death.

To understand a text by starting from the center from where the whole thing starts, the heart, which resonates magnetically outwards to fill and transform a space: the body, the room, the world, and change even the color of the sky.

This is the generosity of waiting. That is, instead of slitting your wrists, instead of pointing a gun at your head, the waiting is the most fallible and generous gesture you can muster up.

This is the dead calm. *La calma chicha.*

That is, you can hear the ringing in your ears, the feeling that something is about to happen, but it is so intensely and aggravatingly calm.

You look around and everyone looks *busy*. They are so *busy*.

Figments of productivity.

Grasping onto a feeling of empathy.

Original feelings lost and other alterations to a soul.

A little bed, and aching.

I'm glad to feel the tremors.

Another landscape substitution.

Or simply waiting for your clothes to dry. To not forget. To linger. To wait.

After all, the most equalizing force in the world is the weather. Under the weather we are equally powerless, equally naive. What the skies bring is up to some *other* force.

That is, today I believe in God.

I mean, if when you look up at the sky to see this you aren't thrown into a sudden state of awe and despair, then I just don't know. I mean, fuck, right?

How are we not devastated daily by the mere sight of the sky? How are we not endlessly blown away by the tides, the designations of objects via language, the feeling of gravel, the triumph of our existence despite the weather?

Can you even recognize how blind you are to everything?

> The mind is able to relax, but in poetic revery the soul keeps watch, with no tension, calmed and active.
> — Gaston Bachelard

Here is the idea: that an image, this image, *this* sky, is different. Different from every other sky on any other day on any other moment in any other time. That *this* description of the sky is different from every other, that *this* poem is different. That *this* resonates differently, a different origin, a different feeling, a different intersubjectivity. The essential *newness* of an image. The *difference*. My sky vs. yours.

Here is the continual problem: the sky. Yes, *that* sky. That mother-fucking sky.

But here's another important thing: I am a vile being and so are you.

This is truer than the color of the sky.

I stop wanting to *think* about things in a categorical or logical way. This is the distance we create now as humans. Intellectualism, intelligence, knowledge — which come at the price of empathy, passion, feelings, suffering. You disagree with me. We make objects of ourselves when we are at our most naive, our most privileged, our most focused point. These points are equivalences. Our most intelligent point is also an equivalence. The focus forgets about the rest of the landscape, the heart, the sublime ecstasy of a kind of felicity that is rooted in tragedy, that is rooted in the sky. Don't forget about the sky. Don't forget about waiting.

The sky, at a point, becomes just the sky. The *I*, another *I*.

You don't see it because you persist in the habits of judgment.

My clothes are in the dryer spinning.

Now here is the task. Think of the vilest human being you can conjure. Now become him. Be possessed by him. Understand him so fully that you *become* him, he becomes you. Here is empathy. You did not understand it until now. Here is the ability to recognize what it means to be a human being amongst other human beings, to recognize both the extreme goodness and extreme vileness present inside each and every one of us, to become the *other*, to let the *other* become you.

Is it possible for you to live without judging everyone else, without knowing you are right about everything? With the realization that you really know absolutely nothing except that there are seasons and to wait for rain? With the utmost acceptance of uncertainty? Is it possible? Is it possible for you to ignore the petty and narrow possibilities of the world for just a moment and recall a little bit of the weather? The sky? The feeling you get when you inhale ocean air? Can you put your hand upon the womb of this planet and feel its resonances and let those resonances become yours? Can you come to understand something other than all *this*?

The poetics of spaces.

The possibility of *understanding*.

You are cast into the world and claimed by certain metaphors. But there is the sky.

There is always the sky.

Remember though that the sky isn't blue.

It is absolutely and irrevocably not blue. It's not.

> The poetic image places us at the origin of the speaking being.
> — Gaston Bachelard

A flicker of soul and silence.

Silence makes a space seem suddenly very, very large.

So when you look at me, quietly, silently, the space of our lives suddenly becomes vast. An eternity in the image that stirs below the surface.

Every morning when I wake up and roll over to see you there, I put my arm around you. You awake slightly, move your arm so that I can rest my arm between yours and your chest. This is the most eternal and joyous of sentences, this moment that occurs differently each morning, but eternally. Like the sky, holding all the devastation and hope in the world in a single look.

It's still morning and I am whoever my dog thinks I am.

It's still morning and you are still here.

Upon some shores will wash up slumbering images of devastation.

Today the sky is shrouded in clouds, is waiting, is enacting the problems of language.

Tomorrow the sky is a mirror, clear and pecked and flickering, subtle gradations of creation and failure, the conditions of life when no one intends to escape.

I drag the memories behind me in a net. I stay where I am. Everything is calm around me and the sky is not blue but it is different every time.

I couldn't translate the space so I reached down to grasp the dirt.

I allow myself to hear the echoes.

Walking home, the hidden memories are like oxygen.

The distance swells. Who is pushing who away? A hold outside the body swells. Holding. Still.

LOS ANGELES

There are many things to say about Los Angeles. Most of these things I will not say because you already know them. Because a singular Los Angeles does not exist and even though this post is titled Los Angeles, being and existing in the city of Los Angeles sometimes has nothing to do with the city itself. One fact is that LA is a completely different city for everyone. If there ever was a city in which every inhabitant could tailor their existence and experience of that city completely, it is LA. Your LA is very different from my LA. My LA from a few years ago is different from my LA today.

A city that draws in shades of light, shades of imagination. An impossible city. A forbidden one. Bluish haze and streets streaming down, bundles of grass. It always feels like the last time.

Days when the sky is as blue as—

As the loss of—

As grieving or falling—

Or, days when the sky is as grey as —

As the insistence of—

As the footnotes above—

Or, when we know that the sky isn't blue at all, that the insistence of blue is the insistence of an existence's perceived persistence, that the insistence of blue as a saturated entity is one that humiliates, concerns, mortifies with each step down the sidewalk, the daydream that phenomenologically becomes the insistence of a snail or a palm tree hovering above everything.

Look at the sky, I say.

I don't see anything, you say.

In this place, it is possible to be surrounded by everyone and to be completely alone. In this place, it is possible to simultaneously feel the effect of urban grunge and filth and beauty, garbage and grime in every alleyway, that smell of shellfish, that look that people give you when stopped at an intersection, to feel all of that alongside a legendary hyphen, the reciprocity of nature, of trees, of dirt, of birds, of air.

One of the greatest things is how many views there are of the city from *within* the city. You can drive to numerous points, hike up to numerous vistas, every view of the city completely different, differing psychological standpoints, differing hierarchies of places, the growth and manifestation of a strange perspective of a city that you occupy, pendunculated beaks of birds that caw behind you.

> But as far as I understand, no one intends to escape. Where would you escape to, and why? Stay where you are. Everyone is calm and in a good mood. Besides, multiple perspectives require the utmost precision of finger, eyeball, and muscle, dragging memory along the word's orbit from one layer of fog to another.
> - Arkadii Dragomoshchenko, *Dust*

Seen from the window of your car, the city is a fascinating series of reflections. Silence doesn't exist except for when you turn up the volume on your radio and then, the clusters of the city that reproduce, everyone's gazes fixed upon *something*, misty haze or smog that remains invisible yet manages to cloud everyone's vision. His acts and omissions. Her acknowledgement. His fixed wound. Her tears. His responsibility. Her burden. His inspiration. Her escape.

Some nights I say something about something happening somewhere in the world.

You sound just like my mom, you say.

It is ending, I say.

No it's not, you say.

Yes. It is.

LA is a moving city, or an immensely fixed one in which we move through, quickly, slowly, meandering, zigzagging, on the same routes, on new ones. What the city looks like is what it looks like when I'm stuck in traffic, when I'm speeding down the highway, when I'm focused on being somewhere on time. That is what the city looks like, threads that exist as paradoxical impressions, transparent, immense, blurred, tattooed over eyelids.

To another. Do you still love me? It may not matter anymore. I don't think it does and it probably never will again.

The thickness of the air, though, that noisy silence that you can only sit in when you are still, this is the opportune and irreducible moment of *being* in this city. Yes, the standard logic and majority image of LA dictates a moving landscape. The trembling half-existence of relentlessly running around, constantly, driving, the view of palm trees and buildings and other streets from your car, the receding day, the sunset in your rearview mirror, the approaching deadline that tangifies time, the music, the outbreaks, the *intention* of space that is only felt when moving through it. But LA sits differently when you are still. When you try to take a snapshot and live inside it, and for a moment, the city doesn't exist at all. It is just you and the space and the sky. Just you and the air and the heat and the breath.

> Immensity is within ourselves. It is attached to a sort of expansion of being that life curbs and caution arrests, but which starts again when we are alone. As soon as we become motionless, we are elsewhere; we are dreaming in a world that is immense. Indeed, immensity is the movement of motionless man. It is one of the dynamic characteristics of quiet daydreaming.
> - Gaston Bachelard

You don't understand my devastation.

That I can feel the pain of both the victims and the perpetrators, the witnesses and the listeners, the bystanders and the actors. I can feel it all and it is heavy, the pain of the world is heavy, and in this city I can stay safe-guarded by the sky. The world will end, just trust what the weather has to say, and in the end, none of these tiny things matter, just the sky and its devastation that will shroud the planet in its love and its glory, suffocate us with its violent breath. I stay up late to read poems by Kenneth Patchen and Jaime Saenz because here is my soul and I watch you sleep and I love you but tonight I feel very far away and I am trying to come back. How do I get back?

I feel compelled to touch you but you are sleeping peacefully and I want to will you to wake up, hold me close, and tell me that everything will be all right. Why don't you tell me that everything will be all right?

Probably because it won't be.

And in many cases, sadness is necessary. Heartbreak is *necessary*.

> there are so many little dyings that it doesn't matter which of them is death.
> - Kenneth Patchen

Let's just say that when you stretch out the transparent layers of this city, it becomes a confession.

The confession isn't the desire for death, though there is that too, but that you miss your mother.

The sun and the heat become irrelevant until you go outside to confront the light.

But in the light there is mother, there is that untraceable wound that began with birth.

The city changes when you do, and the confession is that each and every gesture becomes filled with uncertainty.

The city is so certain of itself, but it confesses that it knows nothing when there is the sky.

It's a matter of taking a few steps back, to trace the wound back to the light, the light a frantic ghost.

Not every panorama is an equal snapshot of this city, yet in the end they are all the same, confessing.

It rained once, a thoughtless nod to the wound of this city.

The neighbors yelling next door don't know to face the silence courageously.

The obligation is to pass the shadow on the sidewalk and to keep walking, to skip the embrace with light.

The proclamation is that you are an individual but in one moment you are part of a mass, in another, a ray of light.

> Man himself is mute, and it is the image that speaks. For it is obvious that the image alone can keep pace with nature.
> - Boris Pasternak

Here is the real dilemma. That so many moments in this city are inarticulatable. My confession is that I try relentlessly and hopelessly to capture moments via images, words. This is all a futile exercise. All of this only ends in failure. But sometimes, inarticulation becomes articulation. That is, the photo I try to take, the one that captures none of the essence that I felt in that very moment when I looked up at the sky and wanted to cry, could have died right there, that the photo instead becomes the articulation of that inarticulatable moment in a way that the evidence can only be a frantic ghost too, a wound, a relinquishing of *everything* into a concentration of *something*.

Let me know that you get this. I mean, photos are an example of this, yes, trying to capture that sunset, that cosmic allusion to all of space and time in the upper light of the sky, that devastating miracle of life that becomes contaminated by so many small things. But other articulations too.

Like: *I love you.*

Words for one of the most inarticulatable of sensations. I mean, this is not the same thing for everyone. Every *I love you* is not equivalent. There is no such thing as repetition in love, yet here are the words that claim, that attempt, that bravely endeavor to signify a specific value via language. This is as absurd as calling the sky "blue," as calling the sunset "beautiful," as claiming you feel "happy." All of these attempts, gravitations, comments: absolutely and most certainly, absurd.

But I say *I love you* and I mean it. I mean *something* that I can't describe but these words are the closest approximation, an agreed upon convention that these words will mean something close to what it is I feel, but what is important is the conjuration of all the other feelings associated with the gesture of the phrase, that when you say *I love you* I can feel this sensation of finitude and eternity in my bones, that I can feel the widening of breath, the threat of paralysis when it all ends, and an entire substantial reality built around you that does not yet exist, will never exist.

When I say *I love you*, I recall the memories of a thousand nights of presence, the limits of feelings at night when I am in my bed, when I am outside, when I pause to linger in a single moment of *existence*. Feelings reveal the taint of past trauma. Feelings become vocality and articulated via gestures. You hold my hand and for a moment, that is *everything*.

Can I confess that you become connected to this city somehow, that this city hardly existed before you, that every sky or sunset or towering building, every glamorous palm tree, every sad one, every reflection of light off a window, every conjured sound, they all begin to match the repetitive vitality of your breath, your touch, your existence. This doesn't have to make any sense. It doesn't make any sense that I know you, that you exist, *here*, with me. I'm not sure where you came from. I'm not sure when I came from either. It doesn't seem to matter, though at some point in my life, these things *did* matter. So many things mattered. What matters is your touch. Your breath. Your body next to mine. Your existence in this city with me. What matters is that suddenly, very much suddenly, I can not imagine life without you. That is what *love* is, perhaps, a complete rearranging of the imagination, a complete infiltration of a subjectivity that seems to defer how images correlate with each other. Suddenly, what matters is the color of the sky. The direction of the stars. The speed of light. Significance and insignificance change places.

The snail.

The engraving upon a pillar.

Quick steps. Slow ones.

Hands.

Moments in space.

The density of the fog.

Distance.

Altitude.

Separation anxiety.

Everything.

I want to experience every shade of light with you. Every shade in between.

I want many, many things, yet also, those desires fade away.

It is all terrifying. One day, this city will swallow me whole, and no one, not even the pigeons, will notice.

VAN GOGH

In the light there is a glimmer that sustains a thousand different images.

In that light, you *were*, and you *endured*.

The painting, as a shield, as a paradoxical inheritance of memory, as obsession, as haunting.

Soliciting a nearness that can only tether itself to texture.

(The texture of the sky is that of fingers widening and reaching for blue, of eyeballs straining to look past and within, of palms outstretched to feel cool and smooth of rocks, of green grass torn out of the dirt, of transparent air breathed back out after a luscious sigh.)

Today is my mother's birthday. She died of a brain aneurysm almost 4 years ago. In anticipation of her birthday this week, and of course for my own interests, I visited "From Van Gogh to Kandinsky: Expressionism in German and France," a special exhibit at LACMA this past Sunday. The day previous, Saturday, I was rear-ended by a car going very quickly in traffic. My head continued to throb incessantly.

And then it rained, most elegantly and necessarily, while I read this line from Kit Schluter:

> The seasons, like languages, don't have rules, but habits: are processes of recovery from the ambiguity of their provenance.

Recently, days are spent contemplating the weather, the sky, the clouds, the direction of the light. Is this cliché? I take the proclamation seriously that perhaps, during these fragmentary and transitory days, days of setbacks and enigmas, it is only the weather that is even worth talking about. Being in a car accident is a jolt of adrenaline, and that adrenaline sustains itself in your body for hours, existence for a while at such a speed that becomes foreign but deferential and gleaned like a detracted downer. But it starts to drizzle, then rain, and fragments that were questions now become dreams, coins of suffering become wet with presence, and everything tastes of whiskey.

So, wandering around a museum, excessively air-conditioned and institutional and full of other people, is an odd experience. You attempt to sit with paintings, to endure and to experience, to affirm and substitute another's perspective for your own, to allow distortions of reality to *become* reality, to notice how reality is articulated by such suffering, contradiction, intention, the heaviness of *seeing*. You attempt to be *alone*, to ignore the magnetism of other voices and people, to allow the cold temperature to awaken those hairs on your arms so that you might have access to another sense in these few, solitary, and reverential moments.

> In poetry, wonder is coupled with the joy of speech… The poetic image is in no way comparable, as with the mode of the common metaphor, to a valve which would open up to release pent-up instincts. The poetic image sheds light on consciousness in such a way that it is pointless to look for subconscious antecedents of the image… Poetry is one of the destinies of speech. In trying to sharpen the awareness of language at the level of poems, we get the impression that we are touching the man whose speech is new in that it is not limited to expressing ideas or sensations, but tries to have a future. One would say that poetic image, in its newness, opens a future to language.
> — Gaston Bachelard

How to describe the experience of standing in front of one

of Van Gogh's paintings. How to describe that indescribable and inarticulatable feeling of wanting to tear up instantly, the impulse to put my hand upon the painting to feel its breath, the desire to feel that vitality, profundity, and suffering coursing through my own veins, to feel that it is already too late to understand anymore than all *this*, to sense new separations between rivers and skies, new connecting threads, new impossibilities envisioned via texture and color. A quote from Kandinsky on the wall of the gallery that he wants, above all, to express: expressionism.

Fire within a firebox.

Clouds within a sky.

Curves along a window gleam.

Limits of vision, outside.

A green sky.

Mere fact of nearness.

Mere fact of distance.

Mere facts.

Wassily Kandinsky in his seminal text *Concerning the Spiritual in Art*, writes:

> If the emotional power of the artist can overwhelm the "how?" and can give free scope to his finer feelings, then art is on the crest of the road by which she will not fail later on to find the "what" she has lost, the "what" which will show the way to the spiritual food of the newly

awakened spiritual life. This "what?" will no longer be the material, objective "what" of the former period, but the internal truth of art, the soul without which the body (i.e. the "how") can never be healthy, whether in an individual or in a whole people.

This "what" is the internal truth with only art can divine which only art can express by those means of expression which are hers alone.

Ali Liebegott in a particularly eloquent post, wrote about her experience in front of Van Gogh's bedroom painting:

When I got to "Le Chambre de Van Gogh a Arles" I stood for a long time. I have always loved this painting. It evokes in me a feeling of calm. As a writer, I too, understand the peacefulness of what the room's simplicity meant to Van Gogh. In addition, his furnishings match my aesthetic. Looking at the mirror that hangs over the small table with chamber pot and pitchers I was drawn to a few vertical brush strokes of color. I felt my eyes begin to tear up surprised to find those tiny bits of color on the mirror. There's color everywhere and I love that he represented it in the corner of the mirror, with little vertical lines, like cat scratches. I can't remember ever crying before a painting before.

About a year ago, Ali Liebegott edited a volume of poems around Vincent Van Gogh. The task of writing something about Van Gogh without writing about my mother seemed impossible. The beginning of my piece:

The piece I wanted to write about Vincent Van Gogh was something that would enact the same kind of emotional travesty that gets thrown onto me whenever I try to look at his paintings, the excess of some kind of psychological & emotional turmoil that has managed to inhabit his works in the form of this thick and heavy residue.

Instead, the only text I seem to be capable of writing involves the image of my mother's death.

Because I didn't know that she was going to die, I said goodbye to a yellow face connected to a corpse's body, already pronounced "dead" fifteen minutes earlier.

The strangeness of encountering Van Gogh now is also the strangeness of being haunted by a ghost, of being haunted by my own failings, to dredge up all the inadequacies and all the joyous moments of a relationship between a mother and daughter, to be reminded of missing someone, of realizing an absence, of a visceral connection with the uncanny colors and bent angles and funny edges that don't seem *real*. They're realer than real.

> Form often is most expressive when least coherent. It is often most expressive when outwardly most imperfect, perhaps only a stroke, a mere hint of outer meaning.
> — Wassily Kandinsky

I try to see beauty and sustain it inside my heart and instead I miss my mother.

Perhaps what most appeals to me about Van Gogh's paintings are how imprecise the brush strokes seem to be, how inexact and how removed from reality, how imperfect and perhaps unobvious, yet, full of intention, genuine emotion, sadness, clarity, puzzlement, wonder, devastation, awe, curiosity, love.

How transitory it all is: art. How devastating. How we are renewed by it and destroyed by it.

One version of reality, of course, is that the sky is blue.

But the sky isn't blue.

It is green.

When we look at the trees, we only see how alive they are by the light swirls in between the static trunks.

What is the intention of a sky?

A neon sky?

Sometimes a hidden face. Is it supposed to be there?

The repetition of leaves. Of color.

To see.

To *see*.

To suddenly understand.

Suddenly I understand.

Looking at "Blue Sea" by Emil Nolde, I think about urgency, about blueness, about the devastation and urgent desire of living. To live is to desire, to be devastated, to love, to be destroyed by it all in the end.

The foolishness of poetry. The reverie.

Let's suppose each brush stroke is an urgent one. Or suppose that each is full of absolute intention, angles, movement, feelings of a raging herd of buffalo. Inside your heart: the water move; your eyes sit and close.

Where is the boundary between blue and green?

Where is the boundary between you?

This is the turning point.

This is the turning point.

Strokes that search inwards. Strokes woven thoughtlessly around us, the texture of forlorn gestures and loved ones.

The dust particles get tangled and then settle.

Sometimes, things just happen in life. They just happen.

Sometimes, things are only revealed after death.

Sometimes, they are never revealed at all. Sometimes, the revealing is the end. It is always and forever now the end.

Sometimes the words *because* she is dead and sometimes they stop and jitter away.

Sometimes her presence is through your heartbreak.

Sometimes, heartbreak.

It is so easy to turn away from feelings. It is so difficult to turn away from feelings. It is impossible. To turn. Away. *Feelings.*

When opportunities present themselves though, let yourself *feel*, no matter how much skin it feels like you are scratching off.

Trust me, it is worth it.

NIGHT SKY

There aren't many things as humbling as seeing the full moon through a telescope and being able to see, the moon: not as the moon you see nightly in the sky above, but as a giant entity, practically breathing, with its craters and textures and shadows, practically gigantic, as you squint and nod, and affirm: *Yes, I see it.*

There aren't many things as humbling as seeing Mars, 55,000 km away, not as that tiny orange-red dot in the sky that you point out nightly, thinking, *Wow, yes, there's Mars*, but through a powerful telescope that allows you to see it magnified, even with its distance, and, to see it moving. Yes, moving, fast enough that the focus needs to be readjusted every couple minutes to keep up with its trajectory and reminding you that the stillness you take for granted, your feet planted upon the earth, that stillness is all an illusion, a grand lie, that it is all just the revenant of the iteration that we have not inherited a deep vale that lets us stand upon fixed choices and fixed terrain, but that every acoustical taint or exclusionary trace will be swung out into outer space and then swung right back at us.

We will be eaten by our own shadows, the living separated from the dead by levels of stardust and guilt, and as accompanying the voice of God, we will barely be able to even glimpse beyond the horizon line so boldly set down in infuriating proximity.

There aren't many things as humbling as seeing Saturn through a telescope, to be able to see a tiny white dot, tiny yes, but recognizable with its rings and glimmer, the unnameability and imminence of that ghostdrawn speck, and entire and giant bulbous rock out *there* and you, so much tinier than that speck, so much less significant, right *here*, holding your breath for a steady glimpse.

Indeed. Look again.

The entire wounded cosmos through a viewfinder.

Feel all that twitches in that recycled body and let it echo a nothing song while you try to look out into something bigger than yourself.

Clouds of deep perfections. Darkened skies with cabinet doors pried open. We insist on being able to see.

Something that hasn't been said but seen. Another version of prayer well-hidden in the darkness.

When you consider the possibilities of writing and language, well, you might as well consider the possibilities of the entire universe.

> In poetry, wonder is coupled with the joy of speech... The poetic image is in no way comparable, as with the mode of the common metaphor, to a valve which would open up to release pent-up instincts. The poetic image sheds light on consciousness in such a way that it is pointless to look for subconscious antecedents of the image... Poetry is one of the destinies of speech. In trying to sharpen the awareness of language at the level of poems, we get the impression that we are touching the man whose speech is new in that it is not limited to expressing ideas or sensations, but tries to have a future. One would say that poetic image, in its newness, opens a future to language.
> — Gaston Bachelard

The sense of endless wonder becomes the most crucial element, the nocturnal dream manifesting itself in the articulations of language that become poetry, and the poet's soul left behind as a phantom in the glimpses of the sun.

These things have been here, before us, before language.

Often, we're just deceiving ourselves.

Quite often.

The various contours of *things* become the contours of *seeing* itself.

What you can see and how you can see it: harmonious configurations of perception, repetition, reverie.

The transformative agency of moving marks upon a moving sky. All of *that* up there which continues to perform emphatically from a script we are hardly given access too, or, like a butterfly's first flight back to a future home, we only hover awaiting the future replication of holes, scaffolding, temptation.

The sky's ambivalence is our prevail.

A roofless world for roofless minds.

When every night I look at the moon, it is, too, a nod, an affirmation. *I recognize you. I know you are there. And I know you will be there after I am gone.*

Perhaps the necessary task is to continue to dream, these dreams that bridge the tenuous and tremendous distances between *us* and *them*, that allow us to approach the infinity of existence, to listen to the discourse of the stars, to listen to the desires of the sky.

Cosmic reveries separate us from project reveries. They situate us in a world and not in a society. The cosmic reverie possesses a sort of stability or tranquility. It helps us escape time. It is a *state*. Let us get to the bottom of its essence: it is a state of mind… Poetry supplies us with documents for a *phenomenology of the soul*. The entire soul is presented in the poetic universe of the poet.

Even in my indifference, the depths of the cosmos find ways to reach me. Reliving the past becomes nostalgia or déjà vu, but also a portal into an *out there*. I lift up my fingers and—

I approach you and move closer.

Reflections open and close, and for a moment, I see myself in your eyes.

You used to be just as you are now. You used to be different.

I persist in standing here, dragging all my memories behind me in a knapsack. My eyeballs are exhausted. Gazes fixed.

Even the shadows seem different and I open my mouth to take a breath but have forgotten how to breathe.

It's all right though because my body breathes for me.

I am utterly calm. The night is utterly calm.

Looking through various viewfinders, to close that distance, to turn back and *see* into the night sky. This is the dream.

When your cigarette smoke weaves tangles around my face and I cough, I turn away to look out the window and find it impossible to separate the night from the sky, to separate this cold from that cold, all of this, all of that, everywhere.

When we're up there walking past the trees and it seems the moon has hung itself on one of the branches, I remember the reverie of a child, lying flat on my back outside, looking up, contemplating the infinity of the universe and my own minimal role in it all.

The trembling reveals the awe has changed but lingers. I can't expose all of my doubts at once, but I'm addicted to something, and even the blue becomes a different gaze. Blue gaze, blue texture, blue speech.

Something is missing.

But I do not have to know what.

INYO NATIONAL FOREST & OUTWARD

Here is the perspective here: nothing else matters.

An encounter at such a high altitude: more than breath, breathing.

A different kind of breath. Looser. Tighter.

Here to witness the breath-taking mountains, the heart-breaking half-empty lake, the pressure on your lungs, the feeling of breathing, the natural processes of erosion, deterioration, death.

The physical weathering that causes rocks and boulders to split apart.

The cold and then heat. Tree trunks fallen over.

Questions of what is or isn't relevant in your life.

Questions of what does or doesn't matter.

Really.

Here is the thing. In a place like this, your perspective changes, widens. Remember single frames of your life back *there* and realize what it means out *here*. Recall gestures of comfort, words spoken, feelings. Here: presence. Here: it all.

Here is the thing. Happiness is difficult. Not just to obtain it, but to be consumed by it. For seconds, moments, hours at a time. It is a privileged part of life to be able to be joyous, even for just a few seconds, to be in love, to be content, to at least once breathe a sigh of relief. But it is also necessary to mourn, to lament, to be disappointed, to be angry, to regret.

It is crucial that we fail. And it is crucial that we succeed.

When you see the half-empty lake, imagine what it would look, you replace the word *would* with *should*, replace *should* with *would* again, see snapshots of lives that intertwine and scenes that seem to belong on postcards, exist *in* nature, away from *that other stuff.* You think about the weather. You are ambushed by a group of deer, fleeting, hopping. You think about life as privilege. As burden. You think about the scale of things. Large. Small. Full of holes. Weather-worn. A breeze that rises up behind your back and cools the sweat on your back.

A hole in the wood and cracks in the boulders. Mishear the wind.

All people are not created equal.

But the sky above, is a gift.

We all live under the same fucking sky.

Hollow rhymes of upside-down words. None of those *words* are matter out here, are barely audible. Direction of water. Thawing solitude. The proximity of retreat and following your memories in your own sleep.

Don't the dreams even make different noises out here?

This is how the world ends: you are sitting on the edge of your bed, head in your hands, crying.

This is how the world ends: a cat meows in the alleyway.

This is how the world ends: flecks of dust illuminated in a ray of sunlight.

This is how the world ends: your arms wrapped around me, the clouds above us pouring down rain.

Gone nothing.

Gone everything.

Here is the thing. People should not call other people evil. Evil doesn't exist, unless the devil does. He might. The gesture of calling another human being evil is the gesture of *I hate you and you are the opposite of me. I am good and you are evil. I am right and you are wrong.*

The assumption that *you* are better than *them*, a simple one, but the inheritance of underserved volition. Actually, you don't know anything. You don't know a single thing.

Polarized categories mean that there is no chance of a middle ground, of understanding, of empathy. Only one side can be right. Only one side can be wrong.

To not be on the *right* side, the *correct* one, fully and completely, without question, is an act of betrayal.

The gesture is an unwillingness to understand another's point of view. To skip empathy and to move on to moral judgment.

That is, the words you have chose to represent you are absolute and finite. They form a parable of differing slivers, the past crumbling down in a backdrop of pettiness (petty bones of petty people being pettily crushed and fed to the birds). Your words don't ache the way theirs do, and so, therefore, the night itself gives into the language of the *correct*, and all other molecules ought to rearrange themselves around the *rightness* of your *correctness*.

Of course any judgment that you are better than anyone else is a godlike gesture. Of course every human being wishes deep down to be a god. I can admit that if I were God I could easily and with the support of "morality" exterminate half of you. Does this scare you?

You see through the window and can't realize that it isn't so. That you are the fray on the golden robe and that you are the one flailing around in circles, unable to even differentiate tides at different hours or stars in the night sky.

Out here, we have a conversation about which hike to go on. This is petty and necessary.

We are cooking dinner and the coals are too low and the grill is too high.

What should we do?

I don't know.

This conversation is also petty and necessary.

And human.

Humanness is not about bravery and compassion, the noble or brave traits of "great" people. Yes, these too, but animals are also capable of compassion, of bravery, of selfless acts of bravery, of love. What makes us different though, is our ability for vileness and judgment. With our "higher intelligence" we create things, the wonders of technology, but we also create more ways to hurt each other, to critique each other, to judge each other. Intention is not always malicious. But it gets muddled with morality and ethics. Intention is not an ethical choice. It is a subjective one, selfish, sympathetic.

We are all capable of good and great things. We are also all capable of cruel acts, of making mistakes, of acting selfishly, of vileness.

What we require on a most base level, is empathy. Not empathy for those we care about and those we already understand (that, of course, is just sympathy again), but empathy for those we villainize most.

We villainize because we don't understand.

And most of understand so very little but operate under the assumption that we understand it *all*.

Foolish restlessness.

Hands holding ice cubes, trying to prevent them from melting by one's own body temperature.

Remember the depths of silt, of water whirling around your ankles.

Remember joy and sadness. Remember rolling down a hill. Remember pain.

Here is the thing. Villainization is also objectivization. Somehow, the standardization of affect has permeated categorization has turned it all into polarization. There are only victims or perpetrators. No longer human beings. Victims, too, are not human beings, but objects, symbols.

The divide is arbitrary and destructive.

Here is the thing. In the end, we are all human beings. This is important. This matters.

Here is the thing. Empathy is crucial.

Yet the burden of empathy is on those capable of it.

Start by empathizing with a tree. Its tenacity and persistence to survive. Think of those trees that grow on the sides of mountains, in crevices, in places no one else wants to go. Trees with initials carved into them. Trees that don't complain and persist, that fall over from wind and storm, that endure after fire.

Think of the empty lake. Trust in nature.

Empathize next with fire. It destroys everything it touches. When it is put out, it fades away, smoke that lingers for a moment to let you know it was there, that it is time to leave. When it is called upon, it puts forth its best effort to destroy, blazing trails and leaving behind ash where there once was life.

Then, empathize with the weather. The slow deterioration of everything under it. Indeed, all narratives are about deterioration but we make them stories about conquest and growth and vitality. Growth exists but as temporary and fleeting. We live in an empire of mud and weather.

Losing sight of *that other stuff*.

Losing sight of *others*.

Tears streaming down your cheeks when your heart is broken.

Tears when you are happy.

In love, effortlessly.

In love, with utmost difficulty.

Here is the thing. There is a responsibility to being enlightened. Being enlightened doesn't mean that you are more intelligent or knowledgeable or passionate or moral or correct. It means you are more capable of empathy.

Ethics isn't about rightness. It is about humanity. It is about failure.

Again, here is the thing. The burden of empathy is on the one who is *capable* of it.

Here is another thing. Just go out there. *There*. Away from *here*. Witness the night sky, away from the city lights, with all of its glittering and endless wonder. Lie down to flatten grass and feel small jagged rocks digging into your back. See the poems emanate from the leaves, the tree bark, the evaporated water, the seeds. Unravel your own moral condensation and stare instead into the eyes of a deer. He will stare back at you.

See with your eyes the echoes of the universe. All of that magnified and so far away, up there in the darkness.

Hold my hand and be with me. *Exist* with me.

Human beings.

Our pasts and futures up there in the stars, our present here, as humans, in the mud, glorious and good, vile and filthy.

Feel like this is the last time.

Imagine that this is the last time.

It is the last time.

What do you remember?

What do you remember now?

SAN FRANCISCO

Sometimes a place is a site of conjuration that sits, welling up, contaminated, voice and remarks reserved for *later*, and the secret self that is *of* the place takes on a pretension of nostalgia, of joy, of beauty.

On grief. On memory. On moving forward.

Here is the thing though. Over and under the light, a bridge sits between points of land. A dreamer is off to a bad start when she is late for her own appointment with the sunset.

A still memory becomes assembled on its own, a series of memories, a heap of ashes that blows away in the wind, scatters, drowns.

Memories don't burn but they fragment, deteriorate, separate and are easily blown away with a heavy breath.

I return to a place of my childhood, a place both utterly familiar through its *essence*, and unfamiliar in its *specificities*. I return to gaze down upon the bay where my mother's ashes are scattered and, do what? I am not sure.

This is a city most beautiful from the outside looking in. No other city takes your breath away the way this one does, as you enter, crossing a bridge and having the city momentously and gloriously grow vertically in front of you as you seemingly circle an entire horizon line to arrive, here, this city of cities, this wound of wounds.

The city is legible as a city, as a dismissal of memories. Many things remain questions here. It is crowded. And the sky becomes deconstructed, designated, something that opens up as you inch toward the margins and exterior lines of this territory. From the center, it is dirty and grimy. On the margins, the fresh air, the breeze. I see the city from this corner, that height, this cliff, that viewpoint. This is the way to see the city and to have its traces, now just dust and ash, creep up into your nostrils via the wind and permeation of thought, the encounter with the phantom that haunts these streets. Speak to it. Whisper. Then take it all back.

I want to enter the city as the sun is setting. To see perhaps one of my most favorite sights in the world, a view that conjures up the ontological difference between life and death while sitting in the car, just looking, *looking*, the orange sky reflected against the skyscrapers that crowd up against each other, the glints of sky-color, of sky-blue, of sky-orange, of fire, of ocean, these susceptible wounds that open up and close and then present themselves in front of your eyes as you move gracelessly into its heart.

The arriving is everything. This *return*. This coming. This ever-after of a journey and the city that builds itself in front of you in a matter of seconds. Once you enter it, that view disappears.

But, I miss my appointment. I nap for too long and when I arrive the sun has already almost set and the buildings look dreary, the night lights not yet on so even the expected evening glamor is missing from this landscape. The too-lack-luster of the too-late.

I try to hide the disappointment, the heartbreak.

It's no big deal. Next time, I say.

(Memory of orange-hue memories upon glass windows upon tall buildings.)

Ok, you say.

It's the revenant that follows me everywhere here. Mine. Yours. Hers.

I do not exaggerate when I say that I have a love-hate relationship with the city. I can't imagine living here. But it is a part of my origin story. And where my mother's ashes rest.

I do not cease hopelessly romanticizing this city and I do not cease battling against its tyranny. This isn't an allusion but just me, in the throes of the haunting, in the paradox of easily forgetting one's mother's face but bursting into tears from the sight of the city while standing on the Golden Gate Bridge.

Standing under the bridge I see the water, blue, deep, teary. That ocean. That bird. That island. That hope. That lost perfection beneath the water, a poem climbing down over the ledge into the frigid liquid below. That personal anguish that is just a part of mourning. That is just a part of *I didn't get to say goodbye so I can't stop telling the air I miss you. I miss you.*

Standing at Land's End, the end of the world on the edge of a peninsula, I see the same water, blue, deep, teary. That ocean. Those waves. That sun. Those ruins. The penetration of a place into the gut of a person. My gut. *If I come back here to swim it'll be as a ghost and I will be dead.*

The fault of the fault line is a promise, unwavering. The denial of salutation is wounding. The necessary gesture is a gaze. Then, to cry. To just cry. There is no other debt to be paid. Just the tears that land cold onto my cheeks as the wind pushes hard. Memory is perpetration. Memory is not unkind. Memory is full of holes and blurry and vision is blurry when there are tears and *I miss you I miss you* but I don't know what to say just *hello* and *goodbye* and *I miss you.*

You perhaps don't know how to fit into this personal mo-
ment. I stop and linger for too many moments at a time and
I say something about *there are my mother's ashes, in there.* You
perhaps don't have words and this isn't your story but you
know to put your arms around me and kiss my cheek and
that is all that I need.

This is all I need from you forever perhaps, the gesture in a
moment to fulfill a lifetime.

I wonder about so many things while driving through this
city with you. I confess that I can't help wondering what
a future with you looks like and I want it. A future. With
you. The contents of my memories spill over and then are
drowned in the bay and what binds me to this city today, is
not the nostalgia, nor even my mother's ashes, but you, here,
with me now, driving up and down these streets, the awaited
conjuration that depends not on the past but a contingent
present and future with someone who has become my entire
world.

We eat ice cream that starts to melt and drip down our
hands instantly from the harsh, focused light of the sun. We
walk through alleyways that smell like putrid garbage and
are stopped in different modes of traffic. At a snail's pace, the
landscape floats by. We reconstruct your favorite shot from
Vertigo at Fort Point and the smile you wear on your face, the
recognition of that familiar, fantastical faraway place, that
smile screams.

Don't let me get too dramatic. But the *I love you* gets tangled
up in all this weather and you take my hand always when it
matters. It matters now. It always matters.

I inherit from the city an impulse to linger. I also inherit from it a tone of continuation and escape. I learn to live *finally*, finally. To identify what it means to go through life not as a writer or a teacher or a friend or a daughter, but simply, as a human being. Is it strange that I feel I've played so many roles and with you these roles don't seem to matter, are irrelevant? And for the first time perhaps, I am just another human being. This isn't a dismissal or a ghosting of identity. This is a relief. An acknowledgement of something else that is magnetic and frequent.

These days everything seems to bring tears to my eyes. I read a line in a poem online. I read something about ghosts. I see water. I see sky. And it is all deeply overwhelming and sad. And yet the visitations of these moments of possibility are also open and full of the work of mourning, which is acknowledgement, which is life, which is continuing to learn to live with *it* and everything else. *Finally*, how to live.

What dissipates when the wind pulls my hair out from behind my ears?

What drowns in the water if not my own body pushed over the edge so easily?

A plunge.

The context.

Visiting a tall place, a cold place, an unfamiliar place on the parapets of midnight.

Continuing to learn to live with *it*.
Continuing to mourn.
Continuing to fall deeper in love with you.

Continuing to continue.

Even if the water is cold and deep. Even if the sky is too bright and the sun burns my skin while I drive. Even if I'm haunting the space more than it is haunting me. Even if I forget everything.

Lapses are what normalize these impressions and even when it seems my heart is foreclosed with the weight of regret or sand, I remember you and everything that has dissipated in the wind and is now just sand or ash or dust.

We will all have the magnificent opportunity to live this fantastic duplicity of ghost and dust, of specter and ash, and when that moment arises, you will have forgotten everything you have ever known and it will be a relief. Until then, I will remember and forget with every fiber of my being and unmute the conjuration of the sky. And I will let myself cry whenever I see it.

She enters the house to see the dog inside. She enters the house to greet the dog inside. She enters the house to be with the dog inside.

She enters the house.

TRAPPED UNDER
THE SKY

Sometimes I am just trapped under the fucking sky.

A speculum of sweating and oath-making, expectations for anomalies, anomalies of expectations.

Many years ago I tried to put something into writing. It became a performance of mourning, then muted, then mutated, then an initiation into another stage of mourning, a steep slope of late-morning haze and tears and learning to pronounce words that describe more precisely the un-blueness of the night sky after the sun had set.

The sun has set.

And here under its cushioning and smothering mania, there is the marbled onrush of clouds. To avoid all the confusion, I stare ahead while driving then snap random photos of the outside with the windows rolled down. The sleep slope leading down to the river, to the shore, home.

I need more words around me.

That was my home once.

How we count clouds and how the words evaporate on paper are not the same.

Writing that bisects the horizon line.

The sky is vast and infinite and impoverished and oppressive and it is awe-inducing and beautiful and petty and devastating.

Here's the thing: I don't know what I want.

I also don't have the energy to keep trying again and again. My heart is sore and tired.

A lot of what is said, I can't ever trust again.

And your words either sting and demolish, or cluster and dissipate. We lived inside each other once but now any thought contaminated with your presence only brings back that dull, throbbing pain.

There is a past that I can't ever trust again, and the devastation of multiple and repeated devastations, the abuses on a heart, just can't ever be forgiven or forgotten. A tennis racket leaning against the wall. Words. That's where I lived once. Among words. And after it all, I am a different person, happy, perhaps, but stretched across this city in a different way.

It is today.

I am glad it is today and not yesterday.

Today I melted in the heat and then was put back together again. Today I clung to hope and then was ravaged by it.

Today I expected nothing and fell flat like the sky, separated sky from water, heat clinging to my skin and a knock at the door like an interrupted scene.

Today we will all linger in our dreams for a little bit longer. We are not ready to wake up yet.

Today the memories occupy this space a little bit differently, and somehow a new and regular presence makes this home a more permanent prospect.

They say that the sea —

Your name doesn't roll off the tongue so easily.

One must sweat first before initiating any contact with a ghost. It is the heat that cements the pact, muted voices unmuted by touch and heat and speculation on the color of the sky.

Last night the sky was stretched out wide, open, moving, laying on the sand next to you as the water rushed loudly and car headlights attempted to break the silence of the sky. We could see the stars and the sky and the stars in between the stars, and in the prolonged gaze upon that vast out-there, we could see it all moving, turning, rotating, blinking in and out of existence.

The sky moves and we tremble. The sky moves and we sleep. The sky moves and often, we don't notice, but when we do, it is a reminder of the promptness of the universe, that it all continues to move whether or not we notice, whatever speed we are moving in our every day.

Can you remember the anomalous quotation marks in the sky, the repetition of stars and patterns that stroked against one another and asked to be connected?

Of course we connected the dots, you say.

How could we not, I say.

And in this exchange more hope and stringing of lights around trunks of palm trees. Listening to Bad Religion and the image of palm trees as candles.

Keep reminding me how you feel. Reminders are necessary.

Highlights of clinging.

A clinging species.

Sand.

Let me know that you can imagine the future too. That I am not alone in hoping for the possibility of a future. That you can see past today and tomorrow and wonder about the beyond. Together.

Let me know that you might walk down that steep slope with me, wherever it goes, and in the cold or heat, letting the sweat cement any words that might be uttered in a gentle breeze.

Remarks repeated. And again, the heat. Trapped under it all.

We are bound by it.

The sky.

And that is all there is to it.

BLIND SPOT

Can you hear blue? That feeble cousin of the voice of the sky that lingers around only long enough to be categorized as a color, then fades away into the memory of language that keeps its petals even after the rare winter rain.

Or, the uncertainty of blue, loud and pervasive in its ever-changing silhouette, in its constant near extinction by the sun, the violent beating of a chest when blue becomes blue becomes not blue becomes grey becomes —

I haven't talked to my father in —

I've been lying low to avoid the —

The tide rushes in, immensely, like a carpet that crawls up my feet to —

In the *sometimes things happen for a reason* we find a reason to doubt the helplessness of others, or to assume it. I wonder if you remember. The questions.

Sometimes the questions accompany us, stronger than any admonition, the temptation to rely on written words digs an abyss, fleeting, empty space that stares back at the maw of your *waiting*. What are you waiting for? Nothing.

But it's just that —

Neither day nor —

The most difficult thing is to —

Every morning I see the same squirrel make its way down the tree, onto the stone ledge, and scramble vertically down below.

Every morning the same squirrel.

Today, the scotoma in my right eye is filled with a white wall. Mostly because it doesn't want to write. Instead, I want to give into desolation. The desert. Instead, I just want to sleep a little while longer. Flung into sleep. Flung into the mourning of mourning.

Arms. Your arms. As a word emerges from the shadows and creeps up your chest, swelling curtains filled with night air, who else is really in this room?
Sometimes happiness isn't conducive to a productive writing practice.

I wonder if I remember.

Her face —

Let's just say the murmur I've been hearing is the question I want to ask you echoed back to me. Because I am afraid. But the fear is taking up too much space and volume. I can see it swelling up as only eternity's desert can, lying flat, cavernous, open. Considering the placid morning. Birds.

Tonight the words don't seem to come together the way I want them to. Is it because I've had something on my mind for the last few days but haven't been able to say it out loud?

I try to whisper them imperceptibly while you are sleeping to see if you might absorb my ridiculous thoughts via osmosis.

But you wake up every morning with the same face, still speechless, still —

More than anything I just —

I can't imagine what tomorrow might look like without you
and I can't stop thinking about our —

When I say that the words don't come together today, I mean
too that they don't come together around you.

Avoidance.

The hesitation to end anything, to say anything.

Or the air that answers the menace of possible responses
with more wandering. Or the rootlike slowness of thoughts
but the strange speediness of feelings, fickle, like burning
paper. Then, just ashes. Just like that.

This seems like a throwaway.

This seems like a distant memory.

An impossible sight:

Some of my favorite views of this city are through my blind
spot mirror.

Palm trees ablaze.

Reddening skies.

Teetering rooftops.

Clouds.

Holding back the soil, the magnified swallow of sunshine.

Its prestige.

The errant signal of looking. For a moment. A moment too long.

The canny, bent blue of faraway, a tranquil but deeply-felt distance.

One thinks that no one will witness the murder they are about to commit. The truth is that the possibility of that violent gesture is what drives one forward. In time. To act. In all aspects of their life. Including the violent ones. And the contributions they might make sitting behind a desk. In a car.

Survival is an obscene gesture. An unnecessary one. No one *has* to live.

Exhalation as privilege.

Fucking privilege.

Oppression as sacredness.

Legibility as devastation.

Identification as sacrifice.

Death as conscience.

Staggering legs.

The results of responsibility.

The results of two lines crossing.

Preparing for autumn. I. am. so. Ready.

For autumn.

Then:
the rows of birds perched on streetlamps.
the indigestion after a spicy meal.
the squirrel.
the darkness that settles as you are driving.
the air.

Forget the words. Just forget all the words for a moment.
Because all of the words are utterly limitless and limited. I
just want to hold your hand. I just want to say good night. I
just want to forget how to write for a little bit and remem-
ber something I used to do as a child, sunlight pouring in
through a window, collecting the suspended dust in the air
with my tiny fingers, stretching my arms to feel...

SUSPENSION OF THE IMAGINARY IN THE REAL

Flickering routes of communication.

Do you see that the memories segregate themselves according to degrees of fuzziness? Dancing across the keyboard. Tides of reflective lines. Flickering.

I remember a moment at the edge of a pier. I am waving to my mother but she is very far away. She is blurry and shiny, like an old photograph. She reaches out and smiles, and then, I only remember wandering through a crowd of people, looking for her.

Moments of exactness.

Fuzzy moments.

Mother asks, *Where did you go?*

I respond, *I don't remember.*

This week I'm teaching Alison Bechdel's *Fun Home* in my class and thinking about the "suspension of the imaginary in the real." When Bechdel uses this phrase, she's talking about her father and the way in which he lived a forced identity that had repercussions on their family dynamic, and his obsession with F. Scott Fitzgerald's stories and their inextricability from Fitzgerald's real life. When I think about this, I think that this suspension of the imaginary in the real doesn't just happen with identity, though this is where we see it manifested very clearly, especially in the ways in which we cope with each other on social media. But more obviously, and perhaps dismissively, the way we construct the world around us, with a hyper-focused magnifying glass, with a bent on anger and outrage, with one eye closed and one eye all too open.

I want to go back and let's just settle on this, that the sky isn't blue.

You will disagree with me, and say of course it is, the sky is very blue.

I will also disagree with myself, look up at the sky in the wake of the daily devastation of movement through this vast and tumultuous city, this heat and grogginess, I will comment on the blueness of the sky.

But in the end, the sky isn't blue. This is a pretense, an illusion, a categorization that functions beautifully, gracefully, doubtfully.

The blue is a signifier of distance, of desire, of longing. The sky is blue because we *want* it to be blue and because it is blue it is very far away, and because it is far away, impossibly so, we want it more.

Fingers can't grasp blue.

But clear water runs down skin easily, transparently.

This is a problem of language. But in the end, that's what it all comes down to, isn't it?

A fortune cookie tells me that I do things with refinement. What a fucking lie, I think.

> This town ain't yours.
> This town ain't mine.
> — "This Town" by Clare Bowen (as Scarlett O'Connor) &
> Chip Esten (as Deacon Claybourne), *Nashville*

There are many truths I have learned from watching TV's

Nashville. One is that being in love is about being with someone that makes you want to be the best version of yourself.

When I accept that the sky isn't blue but that I see it as blue anyway, I also accept that the best version of myself is not the best version of myself that everyone else sees. That is, at the risk of sounding arrogant, the best version of myself isn't a writer, an editor, a genius, a thinker, or any other pre-conceived identity, because, I realize, most of my life I have worked hard to fit into these identities while trying to be outstanding. I have always been an over-achiever because my identity was "to succeed." Excessively. To exceed the expectations of my mother, because her expectations were always to be better than everyone else. And because a large portion of my identity was to be a daughter. A good one.

What I realize is the death of my mother also meant the death of a trajectory towards "success." That I didn't have to be led along an imaginary stairway that led to the next level, then the next level, then the next. At a certain point, I ran out of the levels that my mother had assigned me. Like a platformer video game with no end, I had to be devastated, shaken awake, in order to be able to see what possibilities I could touch outside the universe of the game.

I remember coming to this acute realization while walking in Griffith Park with my therapist. She kept asking the right questions and I conjured the answers. My entire and unshakable mood, the kind of mood where one isn't melancholy or sad exactly, where one is rather content but not happy, where things seem flat but eventful, when apparition becomes substance and vulnerability even is very elusive, seemed to be part of a grander hesitation. The question of *what next*. The question of releasing the ghost of oneself to face another.

In the darkness, I remember sight.

In the silence, I remember music.

In the waking life, the mirror-like images that my fingers can reach out to touch, carefully, deliberately.

Remember, language is elusive.

Remember, language is manipulative.

Remember, language is a frame.

What I realize is that the best version of myself that I have yet known is the person I am with you, a human being, stripped away of these other essences, vulnerable, flawed, emotional, questioning, uncertain.

Between us there are so few words. I am not used to this. I am used to many words.

Extreme and exact articulation. I am a writer. This is what I do.

But sometimes, articulation is overrated. Words are over-rated. Language exists because language fails. But not all communication is built on language.

Sometimes we can just exist, silently, next to each other, barely touching, that *feeling* of connectedness that feels more real to me than words.

Perhaps I'm imagining this, this *feeling* of connectedness. Perhaps I fall in love too easily and I don't see the pretense in my over eagerness to be *happy*.

I doubt everything. I can't help it.
But it is only when I look at your face that I can relinquish my ego in a way I have not been able to do with anyone else.

A projection of two single bodies.

The gentleness of recovering one's past.
The violence of recovering one's past.

When you put your hand upon my leg, this is another route for communication. When, in the middle of the night, you search for my hand, half-asleep and barely conscious, this is another route. Wordless tracks that don't omit words because the words don't exist. Not in this space between our bodies. Not between *this*.

Other times I want the words so bad, like an addiction, words for feelings, feelings for words. More words.

Today I am not feeling well and you make me drink an entire glass of grapefruit juice. My face sours. Then smiles.

In a language I am still learning to understand, I can feel clearly and uncertainly the tenor of your heart.

I use words that are vague and ambiguous because love is vague and ambiguous and because ambiguity can become specificity can become abstract can become precision.

To tell you the truth, when you come up from behind to put your arms around me, that means more to me than any strings of utterly romantic language you could string together.

Yet, I admit, I still crave the words like I crave blue.

In sight.

Watching, through the window.

Essentially, you.

I won't push the words, because you're right. They're just words and sometimes the failure is okay. But when I say "a long time," I mean it, whatever those words might mean to you, tomorrow, later, whenever.

THE COMPROMISED
BODY

"People have always been divided into two groups: victims and murderers. I don't know whether it is possible to free oneself from one group and switch over to the other during one's life. I at least have not yet managed to become a murderer." – Unica Zurn

Sometimes, it is assumed, that the compromised body is weak. Unreliable. Sick. Reaching.

That when something is compromised, one's body, it does not meet the usual standards. It is *lower* somehow. Untrustworthy.

Sometimes it is assumed that the sensory capacities for a compromised body are also lower, weaker, duller. Less.

But if we take the color of the sky as an indication of anything, it is that compromised bodies can *see* differently, and to *see things* does not mean to see things that are not there, to be labeled as hallucinatory, but to see things differently, subjectively, intensely.

I'm saying that there is no such thing as a "reliable narrator" or a "non-compromised body" and therefore no such thing as a "non-compromised text." I'm saying that we all see things differently, it's just that what you see and what I see are similar enough that we can use the same words to describe what it is we are seeing and feeling, but at some point, the similarities will break down.

You will feel cold while I feel hot.

You will see the sky as blue, and I will insist that it isn't.

You will feel absolutely nothing and I will feel sad and very far away.

No one recalls the oblivion of before. No one can even remember what their homes look like anymore. I know the hair on your face but I can't visualize the bones in my own body. I know the color of your eyes but I can't remember what my mother winking looks like.

Words move and swell in the shadows while outside birds are noisily chattering.

I have already written all of this down before.

The cottage smoke is a nostalgic memory but the blanket-white of sadder sounds arrest traffic and you are awake in the fog.

Stumbling.

The eternal emptinesses that bookend these brief shadow flights through the world. The oblivion that haunts our every movement. Our *somethings* shadowed by *nothings*. Our actions stalked by eternal inaction.

Of course I can't forget.

Of course I can't remember.

You pause.

It isn't about *who* but *how*. How bodies are compromised because the assumption is that they are.

Where they are compromised. *Why*.

Throughout all of this, this blaring compromise and the quick and grievous manner in which we choose to live, we wonder about the living skin that composes us.

Am I eating the right foods? Helping the right people? Doing the right things? How many hours a night should I be sleeping?

The spaces that contain the bodies and the bodies that contain us somehow. That we persist is the compromise we have made with these bodies, these spaces, this time, this air we breathe in and out.

Soft and trance-like. Forget-me-not.

In the morning when you wake up having to face the reality of it all and weighed down by the absurdity of doing anything, or even getting out of bed, the outburst: FUCK IT ALL. I GIVE UP.

In the bed when our bodies are lying next to each other and the flesh of me has no words to speak to your body, only the longing, the desire, an arbitrary name drawn in the dust.

Are bird and summer—

That curve—

I can be sadder for you.

The forlorn face of the dog that says, *You can stop crying now.* The forlorn face of the dog that says, *You can keep crying.*

In the bathroom I am collapsed on the floor and sobbing uncontrollably, impossible to breathe and breath only coming with the crying, the crying that makes the entire body ache, the tears the refresh the hot skin and aching, the tears that sting and the world is unbearable right now.

In the car and you are driving and my head is on your shoulder, my left hand resting on your leg, your right hand clenching my right hand. My eyes are closed and the warmth of the sun today is the most beautiful thing I have ever felt.

In the bed and the warmth is only measured by absence and the exhaustion of crying finally forces me to fall asleep.

Life is hesitation. Supper suspended in the air. Endless waiting. Clattering through. *This is what they have done.*

Even the birds, a mystery. What are they looking at?

I don't even remember what I wrote the first time.

Really what we fear most isn't death, but that death isn't the end. That there isn't an appropriate end to an appropriate narrative.

Shame comes with time. With mortality. The shame of being and aging and the brevity of it all.

Why is getting lost simultaneously such a burdensome and a beautiful relief?
I want to get lost with you.

That is all there is this: relief. The relief: that this is all there is.

Mortality is a relief but not a promise.

There are no promises. Only compromises.

Calmly, serenely—

And often now—

While the birds—

The birds.

Believe me, the sky isn't blue today.

Sometimes the sky is blue just because you need it to be.

Sometimes it doesn't fucking matter.

Sometimes I remember the singing. Sometimes I don't see anything.

If the stars could weep I would let them, hold them in my arms and let the suffering happen because the suffering is needed sometimes to see how crying relates to horror to sorry to world to tenderness to *there*.

I only ask that you hold me when I am weeping. It won't be quiet or brief. But it will be necessary.

I want to be alone with you.
Why are you never alone with me?
Or when we are together, alone, we are also very far apart.

In the mornings I am thrust back into the world.

A moment later you are holding me.

The kitchen light is still on.

Landscape as recourse as —

Let me show you.

OUTER SPACE

I don't know.

No, it's a long story.

I tried to leave but couldn't.

Somehow, I found the motivation.

Not everyone will be taken into the future, but everything depends on it. The future. Our imagined version of it. All of this is because the future seems to exist in some way and there will be no repeat.

One: *I shall not be taken.*

Another: *I can't wait.*

Another another: *When do we leave?*

In one moment, it seems that everything is responsive to my every move. That is, before I can bear any judgments, I am adventuring in my head just by existing under that sky. The enormity of all of *that*, that is, the madness of it, the aberrant nature of sky that you stare at longer and longer until it blurs together, until more lights appear, until you can see that entire enormity of possibility start to spin, slowly, eternally, the power of light that reflects intensely, necessarily.

Movement.

Slow movement.

How to impose a poetic order on that night sky? From down here, none of it is completely ours. Only the distinctness of new beginnings that are already endings. That is, you see a star being born, and by the time you have seen it, it is already dead and absorbed into your very being.

From up there, the blaring glare of silence, the witnessing of archetypes being born. Mirages of nostalgia. An endless zone of regrets.

Why would I remain here?

I'm scared.

What I fear more than anything is being alone.

For me, it is important to just exist.

In the brightly lit darkness, dialogues with the dead.

The reshaping of a kind of communication that can elicit marvel.

The broken down quality of an archetype that doesn't know how to restart. That is, in the memory it is always blue.

But hyphens are pauses, and the poor dreaming self is still hiding behind the memory of a color that was never seen. Lost.

I realize how charged I am with hesitation, that this is what drives everything, the echo of heartache that lingers over everything I love. The more I fall in love, the louder that echo, the closer that thud, an exaggerated poetic impulse that is as natural as smothering your lover alive in his sleep.

I realize how the language gets put away each night, how the stars absorb the phobia of inner space even when I forget to look up, prevents me from smothering myself and forces my body into compulsory shaking, a shut-down of senses that opens up a horizon for new and deserved breath. Enough is enough. Again, breathe.

Too much space smothers me, convinces me into thinking what an open space I am moving through, that there is not enough certainty to fill this vastness, the oppression of freedom, the illusion of space. Fibers live on.
Because your eyes have been closed.

A landing site for eyes.

Wow, it's all so different!

Is it continuous?

I have been very unhappy with myself.

It was only in my imagination.

For me, it's important to feel.

So that the bent-blue of one sky elicits the dynamism of the cool-grey of evening, that unfaltering chill that comes with an ardor of words. I live on at ground level and we hold hands, heels digging into the ground and looking up at millions and millions of fires.

From up there, looking down, the menace of wandering, the manifestation of new cosmic slowness, rootlike, with no ground for roots to take root, hard wood texture a memory, so, too, the color blue. One takes shelter in the imagined ash of dead beings, sleeping, a slight shock that wakes you when the metaphor becomes too much or is inadequate for flight.

Classified thinking.

Pointing out what is wrong in your argument.

Not caring about the register of objects, but the tremor of voices.

I am speaking. I am speaking.

The absurdity is that you can not hear me.

HOME

> The process of dying is part of living.
> — Dr. Drew.

The thing is, that sometimes the feeling of a moment slipping away is like pointing toward the movement of a finger or an indexing of aging, slowly, though often, the light seems to be in the way.

You used to be just as you are right now once, in a difference place, at a different time, the dragging persistence of self.

Home is where the dogs are.

The heartbreaking sight of your dogs' forlorn faces as you pack up and walk out the door.

Then, while driving home, looking into a brightly lit bus to see all the sad faces, all the old faces, the smiling face of a girl, laughing, the blank face of a man, seated, and this seems somehow a beautiful sight.

Then, the rising moon, shy and yellow.

What the sky looks like proportional to how often you cry.

The moon is hiding from me.

And then, something as silly as Linkin Park's "In the End" playing on the radio to springboard you into an urgent and devastating nostalgia.

Is *this* living?

Is this *more* or *less* functional than being a zombie? That is, is it okay to spend more time *feeling* and *crying* rather than *working* and *doing*?

In my own eyes, what is the eventual outcome, the eventual fate of all of these movements?

Toy soldiers that speak. They seek out the Gorgonite scum.

The sad and forlorn Gorgonites. They seek a home.

Just because you can't see it, doesn't mean it doesn't exist.

Wiiiind.

Yes, the wind.

One's relationship with their house is a look at their intimacy with that space.

That is, I am *on my way* home, yet it is uncertain *where* exactly I am on my way too.

That is, my home might be in transition, several different spaces in a short period of time. So the space that holds my bed? My books? Where I get changed in the morning? Where I brush my teeth?

How long have you lived in your home? What makes a home a home?

Home: where the silence asserts itself like a person, loud and daunting, the silence that is frightening and a comfort. Here, asleep. Here, the attempt to sleep. Where insomnia is at its most intimidating.

Home: where familiar arms hold you. That feeling of being

there with a person, the slanted streams of light that enter in the morning, the buzzing of power lines, the familiar cold that embraces you. Here, the privilege of an extra blanket and the privilege of lying in your arms. Crossing into beyond. Night.

> The universe comes to inhabit the house.
> — Gaston Bachelard

Sometimes, I'm lying here and I can feel it all stretch out around me, a flat and thin outline that permeates through and the space becomes very empty, very full. Here, I remember my mother and many childhood spaces, this deepness of memory and grief: there are currently no photos of my mother in my room. Yet in my room I most often remember her, most often lie in my bed holding the stuffed animal dog that I got for her once when she was in the hospital. One of its ears is chewed up and extra floppy from when she let my dog play with it.

He's going to chew it up, I said.

It's okay, she said.

In a home, everything is transparent and undiscoverable. That is, you enter a person's home and you have the distinct feeling that it is growing. You breathe in a strange vapor while in the heat, you feel the desire fill the space like your lungs during a run. At others it is cold, and it feels like there is a lack of love. You have the urge to rearrange everything, and then, to turn on the heat or light a fire.

At home, you can't help but try and counter that constant shadow of heartbreak or relief. You realize how your home is filled with things that are quite useless, but these things help you *function* somehow and the element of unreality is what keeps you going anyway. The home is mythical. It might not exist at all. In your dreams you're always in the wrong house anyway, or it's thwarted or morphed somehow.

How the deformed version of a home becomes the dream becomes your hands becomes the breath breathed out by you when uttering words becomes hands searching for another body during the night becomes standing on the sidewalk in the mist of rain becomes *I am not dead, yet.*

The convergence of an entire reality and the absence of other versions of homes becomes a spectral longing. I long to put the pieces back together but they don't exist anymore. I long to see my mother but she doesn't exist either.
Most days, the technological implements I touch are the most real evidence that I exist.

I'm used to lingering and waiting for you.

But if a house.

We hover.

Is better built.

The oscillations reverberate.

At home.

Why are you never alone with me?

That's just it.

I just want to be alone with you.

AFTER RAIN

After rain: the perpetual anticipation of the next rain.

Some time has passed since the last time I sat down to think of this irreducible experience, that is, when I see the horizon line burning, that sunset in my rear view mirror, the glimpse of any fire or summoned disintegration of sadness, to tears, to tension, to death's face, to *this* again, when this paralysis of entombing emotions happens, I think of you.

The orange-red-pink sky is burning down.

It is almost nighttime.

I am waiting, for you.

There are the little moments. That is, even if the world weren't so gruesome, it would be those little moments that would carry us through, phantom whispers of joy in joyless times. I see the horizon line burning. I think of you. The moon is behind the clouds. White fluffy ones that veil and encourage the moon's shimmer. Like that pixelated glare behind the curtain when you wake in the morning to, well, *wake.* That is all one can do sometimes. Simply: to wake.

> To look at the sea is to become what one is
> - Etel Adnan, Nightboat Books

After rain: the blue that is left over, that lingers, that breathes anew.

After rain: the sky in the rear view mirror, the little moments, "Stairway to Heaven" playing on the radio, the crescendo, the birds, and why.

After rain: the so-much that is blue, so far, so unreachable, so present, its flickering noticed only via distance.

After rain: the crisp air that taints my lungs with blue, that lies beneath, that immovable, impassive sheet.

After rain: you, alone, you, here.

After rain: the impenetrable sadness of all *this*.

That is, I'm driving in the car, singing to Nashville's "<u>Nothing in the World Will Ever Break My Heart Again</u>," and I'm crying though I'm not sure why, and somehow it seems that all of the sadness of my entire existence, all of the sadness of the phantom individuals that have dipped in and out of my life, all of the sadness of my mother, the sky, the world, it has all caught up to me in this moment and the harder I cry, the more I can't stop singing, and the harder I sing, the more I can't breathe and the density of the tears that fall. Because somehow in this moment, I have managed to condense the entire world's heartbreak into my own, and I can still remember your voice when you said those things that I already forgave you for, and when I look up I see the rows of birds perched up on the wires and the tears come more quickly, happily, urgently, willingly.

Why is the company of birds such a reassurance?

Why under the scattered light of this vast and beautiful and miserable city, why the birds, sitting, bring forth that naked smile that only the birds can bring?

Once, I stared into death's face but he didn't return the stare.

Once, I lay my head on a stone but the shadow above me was too heavy to support and I had to give in to the weight of it.

Once, I summoned the ghost of my mother but was too ashamed to look her in the eye and left her there standing, expectantly.

Once, I remembered that I loved you and wanted to try harder, that I was willing and desiring to reconcile my deepest flaws and failures and insistences for you. That I wanted to be with you, that I didn't want it to be easy, that I wanted it to be whatever it would be, with you.

Once, I could have walked away but I didn't.

> In blue
> nowhere there's
> a game known as
> decay
> — From Wallless Space by Ernst Meister (Wave Books)

After rain, we already know that it all looks different. This city, you, me. Rain changes everything and we only know to keep deferring moments until the next time it rains. When it rains, the people in this city seem to be in perpetual deferment. The clouds that move as the rain refuses to abate, the rain lasts for as long as it lasts and no longer, and *during* the rain, it either feels like a single, glistening moment or like a deeply black eternity. I wonder how wet I can get before I am filled to the brim. Because of the weather, plans change and so do my eyes. I can't tell colors and it's raining all over the place and I just want to sit down in a puddle and soak.

After rain, no matter how torrentious it might have been, we wonder where did it go: the rain. How could it leave us so quickly? The air is thick. No. It isn't. It's rather thin now. And all the bodies that accumulated inside of houses, under rooftops, slowly stumble out and blink and stutter. After rain, we stutter.

No. After rain, we wait.

The poetics of spaces is the poetics of bodies *in* spaces.

The persistence of words, that the words come and express themselves when articulation seems impossible.

How the light is capable of exorcising all your past and present affirmations. The baroqueness of language when it *tries*.

YOSEMITE NATIONAL PARK

That's all there is, isn't it? He said.
Yes.
Are we going to die now?
No.
What are we going to do?
We're going to drink some water. Then we're going to keep going down the road.
— Cormac McCarthy, *The Road*

The precipice of an unending evening, laid out before you.

Of course, we don't mourn the same way we used to.

An impromptu trip that spurns a series of dreams, rich in color, hard and rigid and compressed and preserved in rock. The vertical slopes are majestic, like cathedrals constructed by Gods that aim to reach the heavens.

We walk down the slope. It is steep and covered in moss. Evidence of glacier movement and my shoes, for instance, become for a moment immersed in time. We expect to hit a cliff and then be forced to stop our descent.

In the first view, more rockfaces, elegant. And trees.

In the second view, things are much more complicated. There is a waterfall that we can see across the gap, tiny moving cars.

We continue because we do not reach a cliff. Instead, the rock that continues to cut in and around itself, tiny cracks that split massive boulders, we continue down.

This is a story about descent and breathing. She was descending down the rock cathedral when she suddenly felt awe enter her through her diaphragm, a sensation that would remind her of being flattened. She saw the tiny ridgeline of trees and the sharp edges of rock against the sky, against the imminent death of a misstep.

To say "time passes here" is an understatement. To use words like "immense," "expansion," "massive," "glacial." To enter a habitual phase of regular phrases used in carefree succession is almost disrespectful.

It is so obvious out here how we move around on such a fixed axis of assumptions. The weather is lifted outward and the air, temperature, utterly different and sharp, like the day cleansed by rain but there is no rain and there will not be.

To make lights with fingers, tattered threads of sunlight that waver majestically between eye movements, sentences without subjects or verbs, just wild gesticulations and attempts to restore balance and actualize movement around the silence.

I lay my head down upon a rock, feel the sheer hardness of the rock supporting me, weighed down by the silence, alone for a moment, the day begins now.

I am surprised to see that the stranger who approaches from between the trees is you.

Beyond: sparely scattered clouds. What are you imagining?

In bed you turn over and search for my arm, find it, and hold it around your chest tight.

Good night, I say.

Did you say something? you ask.

Did you fall asleep already?

No. I'm somewhere.

I don't know what will happen tomorrow but I do what happened today.

Is this all, beautiful? This *all* before me. Is that the word to describe it?

In this sacred place, the *then* and *now* exist, produce duration, together, shadows of trees and weather.

You want so much to encounter a bear.

I want so much to understand the value of something written. That is, the moment I am touching the rock is a moment, from memory, then words. Mere words.

Can you even feel your hands trembling anymore? Can you feel it at all?

Close your eyes and remember what the birds looked like before. Repeat the words that describe the birds over and over again. Without the words, the birds still persist. Without the words, the birds still matter.

I pick up a loose piece of moss and find it, as John Muir described, hitched to everything else in the universe. At the center of it all, this piece of burnt-green moss.

Walls of a celestial city we attempt to drive around to witness it all, the sunset upon us and some kind of urgency to *see* it all. But we feel so small down here under those mighty walls, and the light bounces off each edge and corner uniquely, an ethereal stream of light and conscious frivolity.

I am *here* and that changes nothing.

The light colors the sky from certain angles, and when the car is pointed in one direction, radiant murmurs and colors, and when the car turns out of the bend, I turn my neck and stretch in an attempt to see those colors longer. But glimpses, too, choose their own duration, and none of the sky was ever mine to own so I long for more yet understand too that I can only see what I am given, a strange and generous allowance of the sky.

This was a trip that began in spontaneity but the pull of the mountains is strong. My trunk is already stocked with a tent and supplies.

We could stay for one more day.

We have to get back.

I have a tent already in the car.

We do.

Can I see where we are on the map?

Yes, we're right here.

We have to leave because duality is not something we do well. And there are creatures waiting for us somewhere us.

We drive through a long and cold tunnel. I try to hold my breath but I am unable. This isn't a failure but a simple fact of inability.

But the breath itself haunts my memory.

It is impossible to assemble the pieces of a space this vast into anything cohesive. As soon as I focus on a leaf, the waterfall disappears. And as I gaze up at the sky, the entire terrestrial world below just a memory.

It is getting dark.

It is a shame that we can't ever stay in one place.

It is a shame that sometimes people wish they would die.

The weather hasn't been the same in years.

But inside bodies, we look for insistence and persistence.

And sometimes we are able to find it.

GIBBON CONSERVATION CENTER

One of the greatest joys I have ever experienced is listening to the singing of gibbons. Primal and guttural: what would it be like to wake up to these sounds?

In bed, the displacement is not of bodies. Your body is always there, but something else is very far away.

Through the window, still a gray sky, yet the ocean is very far away.

How happy to be able to exist without needing to "win." But we all always want to win.

To win *anything* comes at the cost of humanity. That is, among the gibbons, winning is not about "winning" but about who makes the last sound, the persistence of tone, of mouth open, of song, of life, of being, of last yelp or deep bass or throat-clearing heft. Then, accompanied by the obstinate glances, the crepuscular song closes as it should until prodded on again tomorrow, and the day after tomorrow, and the day after that.

The new slogan of this new life, the one that begins in the middle of a fascist trajectory toward the occupation of equality, is the necessity to call out each other, ourselves: I am a failure and so are you. You are a failure and so am I.

Let's talk about the ways in which we have *failed* each other.

Because failure isn't in that *other* we so preciously push away, but in the allegiances we make during the day and the assumptions we hold onto at night, those assumptions about ourselves that we aren't able to articulate fully as mere words.

Because words are not useful today and because there are so

many words.

Because we know nothing about objectifying our own conditions, only those of everyone else.

Interior rain.

Eyes closed.

There is a nothingness in the will behind every action, the fog of the exterior slowly lifts and bodes are brought together.

It is a joy to watch the gibbons eat. Just eat. One holds on to a green bean between his toes and snacks on a piece of celery while watching us.

He knows we are watching him but understands that he is watching us too. We are not as mysterious to them as we think.

Can I talk about how heartbreaking this all was? That is, a gibbon chewing happily on a vegetable and how that brings tears to my eyes.

Can I talk about how magnificent? That is, several gibbon families all asserting themselves through song, the various melodies and choruses of different bloodlines mingling to create an immense affect and operatic jubilee, how this auditory and visual spectacle that takes my breath away, the tears now coming uncontrollably.

I don't understand why the tears come in moments like these. The gibbons are absolutely beautiful. I am so happy to be here. And yet I don't think anyone else here understands how *important* this is, all this, them.

What we see.

What we cherish.

Hardly an event.

Hardly an encounter.

Do you remember when people used to still ask each other questions?

Do you remember when people used to still sing?

None of what we do is clear to me anymore.

But the delight in unity, separation by caging, the *sounds*, the sounds become the plotlines and even as my eyes necessarily close, those reverberations of tradition and sincerity and persistence continue.

THE DOGS

A black and blacker ocean beneath a blue-black sky.

On the coast, white foam that bristles upwards as the tide rolls in. The ocean: thin, merely stretching out for infinity, merely unseeable, unknowable. Yet something happens. Something always happens.

When I write words in the sand, the water washes away the words in the sand.

When I write the words on a page sitting in the sand, the wind covers the words with sand.

Is *this* the state of things?

How are my memories different as the tide rolls in from the memories that surface as the tide rolls out?

At the moment, what matters is that the dogs beside me are cold. They are breathing in the exhaustion of ocean air, sand in their beards, and stunned by windy whispers beneath their chins.

A different approach as dreams move across the waves and hit bodies. These dreams used to mean nothing to me.

Only, the location of the moon.

Darkening lines and signs of a twilight yet to come.

Aren't we compelled to remember things over and over again?

Nothing remains intact under the increasingly heated atmosphere, advocates of forward momentum but the pronouns are equally fascinating.

The dogs bark from inside the home.

The home, inhabited equally by air and bodies, creaks and moans under the weight of the wind.

The dogs lift their heads at a sudden noise.

A hand turns a doorknob and the dogs bark. Who is entering their home?

The air owns the home more than the dogs do, but the air is silent, complacent.

The gestures of dogs are translated into empathizable ones but when they cry, they cry, and when they sleep, they sleep.

The dog barks because he is scared.
The dog barks because he doesn't like you.
The dog barks because he is alarmed.
The dog barks because he is sending a warning.
The dog barks because he wants to be heard.

The dogs do what they're told, or so it seems, but at the risk of distorting sincerity into honesty, we breathe.

The dogs breathe better when their master is home, the breath using the air built up in the space over the course of prolonged time.

The dogs have been at home for an unspecified but pro-longed amount of time.

The master knows how to keep time but for the dogs, time

has simply passed.

When the master breathes, the dogs can follow, and breathing becomes knowable again.

The bodies become knowable to the other bodies.

When the dogs breathe loudly and calmly, the master breathes a sigh of relief, because their relief is her relief. And in the home, the breathing bodies huddle close together for warmth, the gray sky yet looming outside the window.

The master wonders if and when it will rain. The dogs know that it will undoubtedly rain at some time in the future.

The master wonders what the dogs are watching for outside the window at night.

The dogs are just watching the outside of the window at night.

In every story there is a home and a dog barking.

This story starts with a dog barking inside a home, and then the reader asks, why is the dog barking?

The dog is barking because he is scared.
The dog is barking because he doesn't like you.
The dog is barking because he is alarmed.
The dog is barking because he is sending a warning.
The dog is barking because he wants to be heard.

In every dog there is a strong and urgent desire to love and to be loved.

The incapacity of humans to be their primal and sincere selves is the incapacity to inhabit the dog the way the air occupies the home.

We only know to coddle the dog and to love the dog as a dog, or, in some cases, as a child.

But a dog is more than just a dog, and we are mere humans.

When an airplane flies overhead,
to the dogs: a noise.
to us: an airplane that has just taken off.

Contours of a personal narrative include time, character, space.
But also hair, fur, noses, sand.

Points of transition into *others*.

Modes of being.

The gray sky above us.

The dogness of dogs as having hardly anything to do with dogs.

Consider the quiet of the morning and then the sound of two dogs breathing.

Consider the darkness of night and then the light of the moon only minimally obscured by the moving clouds.

A dog's head on your leg is all the love you need, all the love in the entire world.

One dog places his paw on his master's leg because he knows this is the thing to do.

The master wonders how the dog knows what she needs right now, another warm body that affirms her existence, placates her need for something.

The other dog walks over and yawns, then curls up next to her other leg.

The master wonders whether the dog is cold or sleepy or lonely.

The dogs wait for the master before going to bed because in this house the bodies sleep together and it is nighttime when it is observed as such by the master.

The master persists because she has the dogs and their love is heavy and beautiful and she knows to persist for them.

The dogs persist because they know to persist because that is all they know.

The dogs are sleeping because they are tired.
The dogs are sleeping because their master is sleeping.
The dogs are sleeping because it is night.
The dogs are sleeping because it is time to sleep.

The dogs are dogs and they sleep because they sleep and they breathe because they breathe.

For her own part, the master tries her best to not make any more mistakes.

Sometimes I wish I could die.

Do you?

Yes.

What stops you?

From killing myself? It's not so simple, is it.

It could be.

I can remember regret before it has even happened.

You won't feel regret if you're dead.

That is the assumption, isn't it?

OFFICIAL

CCM ◉

GET OUT OF JAIL
* VOUCHER *

- -

Tear this out.
Skip that social event.
It's okay.
You don't have to go if you don't want to. Pick up
the book you just bought. Open to the first page.
You'll thank us by the third paragraph.

If friends ask why you were a no-show, show them
this voucher.
You'll be fine.

- -

We're coping.

◉

CPSIA information can be obtained
at www.ICGtesting.com
Printed in the USA
FSHW012000241121
86475FS